Physical Character
Italian Spi
(from The Kennel Clut

Body: Length equal to height at withers, chest broad, open, well let down. Topline, a very slight slope from raised withers to well muscled loins, slight rise from loin to broad and muscular croup, croup sloping.

Tail: Thick at base, set on as a continuation of croup line, carried horizontally or down, customarily docked to half its length.

Hindquarters: Thighs long, broad, muscular and strong. Hocks well let down.

Colour: White, white with orange markings; solid white peppered orange, white with brown markings, white speckled with brown (brown roan), with or without large brown markings.

Size: Height: dogs: 60–70 cms (23.5–27.5 ins); bitches: 59–65 cms (23–25.5 ins). Weight: dogs 34–39 kgs (75–86 lbs); bitches: 29–34 kgs (64–75 lbs).

Feet: Front compact, round. Hindfeet slightly oval. Dewclaws on all four feet.

Italian Spinone

◇

By Richard Beauchamp

CONTENTS

PUBLISHED IN THE UNITED KINGDOM BY:

INTERPET
PUBLISHING
Vincent Lane, Dorking, Surrey RH4 3YX England

ISBN 1-903098-96-3

PHOTOGRAPHS BY ALICE VAN KEMPEN
with additional photos by Norvia Behling, TJ Calhoun, Carolina Biological Supply, David Dalton, Doskocil, Isabelle Français, James Hayden-Yoav, James R Hayden, RBP, Carol Ann Johnson, Bill Jonas, Dwight R Kuhn, Dr Dennis Kunkel, Mikki Pet Products, Phototake, Jean Claude Revy and Dr Andrew Spielman.

Illustrations by Patricia Peters.

The publisher wishes to thank all of the owners of the dogs featured in this book.

First and foremost a hunting dog, the Italian Spinone is a reliable pointer, well suited to most any terrain. He is an intuitive hunting companion with unending loyalty to his master.

ITALIAN SPINONE

ORIGIN OF THE BREED

Working side by side with your favourite canine hunting chum in the field or lounging with him in front of the hearth reveals how well the dog has been integrated into our human lives. Certainly the last thing that picture would bring to mind is the wild ancestry that stands behind each and every dog, regardless of its size, purpose or country of origin. It is a well-established fact that, aided by various steps and crosses, all breeds of dog have descended from *Canis lupus*, the wolf, particularly from the branch of the family known as the Northern European Grey Wolf.

How long it took for the wolf to move out of the forest and into man's cave dwellings is a point of conjecture. However, it seems obvious that observing wolves in the hunt could easily have taught early man some survival techniques that he was able to use advantageously. It goes without saying that the wolves that could assist man in satisfying his need for food would have been most highly prized. As the man-wolf relationship developed through the ages, certain descendants of

> ## ANCIENT DOG GROUPS
> As early as the first century AD, Romans had classified dogs into six general groups: House Guardian Dogs, Shepherd Dogs, Sporting Dogs, War Dogs, Scent Dogs and Sight Dogs. Most dogs we know today can trace their ancestry directly back to dogs from these groups. A good many other breeds were developed by combining two or more individuals from those original groups to create yet another 'breed.'

these increasingly domesticated wolves began to assist in a myriad of capacities that ran from hauling to sounding the alarm when a marauding neighbour or beast of prey threatened.

Through the centuries, due to man's intervention and manipulation, many descendants of the original wolf stock underwent significant anatomical changes. In *The Natural History of Dogs*, authors Richard and Alice Feinnes trace the descendency of all breeds of dog from one of four major groups, each of which traces back to separate and distinct branches of the wolf family. The four classifications are: the Dingo Group, the Greyhound Group, the Northern Group and the Mastiff Group.

Each of the groups has its own particular characteristics that have been handed down through countless generations to our modern dog. These characteristics have become the features that individualise and specialise our pure-bred dogs of the day. As we trace back into the history of man's hunting companions, we find a common denominator in the Mastiff Group. This group owes its primary heritage to the Tibetan wolf (*Canis lupus chanco* or *laniger*). The great diversity of the dogs included in this group indicates that they are not entirely of pure blood, as many of the specific breeds undoubtedly were influenced by descendants of the other three groups. The descendants of the Mastiff Group are widely divergent but are known to include many of the scenting breeds. These are the breeds that find game by the use of their olfactory senses rather than by sight, which is to say that they rely upon their noses rather than their eyes. They include the breeds we now classify as gundogs and the true hounds or scenthounds.

As man became more sophisticated and his lifestyle more complex, he learned that these descendants of the wolf could be bred in such a manner as to suit his specific needs. Often these needs were based upon the manner in which man himself went after game and the terrain in which he was forced to do so. The importance here is that man had taken control of the individual dogs that mated. Particular characteristics were prized and inbreeding practices employed to perpetuate these characteristics.

One type of hunting dog that man developed retained the wolf characteristics of pursuing the prey until it was cornered and killed, until it was chased up a

GENUS *CANIS*

Dogs and wolves are members of the genus *Canis*. Wolves are known scientifically as *Canis lupus* while dogs are known as *Canis domesticus*. Dogs and wolves are known to interbreed. The term *canine* derives from the Latin derived word *Canis*. The term 'dog' has no scientific basis but has been used for thousands of years. The origin of the word 'dog' has never been authoritatively ascertained.

BRAIN AND BRAWN

Since dogs have been inbred for centuries, their physical and mental characteristics are constantly being changed to suit man's desires for hunting, retrieving, scenting, guarding and warming their masters' laps. During the past 150 years, dogs have been judged according to physical characteristics as well as functional abilities. Few breeds can boast a genuine balance between physique, working ability and temperament.

tree or until the dog gave up in exhaustion. This practice is more or less typical of that group of dogs known today as the hounds. While the tenacity was held in high regard, a hound's willingness to chase could continue on for miles if need be, and some men found keeping up rather tiresome.

Thus was born a need for the hunting dog that never followed through with the chase or the attack. Its job was not to do the hunting or killing, but rather to assist the human hunter by finding the game and indicating its discovery to the hunter quietly so as not to scare away the game. Further, like any good assistant,

THE POINTING BREEDS OF EUROPE

Great Britain	Pointer
France	Braque d'Auvergne, Braque d'Ariége, Braque du Bourbonnais, Braque Dupuy, Braque Français, Braque St. Germain, Korthals
Spain	Perdiguero de Burgos, Perdiguero Navarro
Portugal	Perdigueiro Portugues
Germany	Weimaraner, Pudelpointer, Stichelhaar, German Shorthaired Pointer, German Wirehaired Pointer (Drahthaar)
Italy	Bracco Italiano, Spinone Italiano
Belgium	Braque Belge
Denmark	Hertha Pointer, Gamle Dansk
Czech Republic	Cesky Fousek
Slovak Republic	Dalmatian
Hungary	Hungarian Vizsla

Braque du Bourbonnais.

Pointer.

Braque St. Germain.

Perdiguero de Burgos.

Perdiguero Portugues.

Braque d'Auvergne.

Bracco Italiano.

Cesky Fousek.

Braque Français.

the hunting dog obeyed its master's commands without hesitation.

References have been made to the existence of this kind of dog as early as the time of the ancient Greeks. Written records point to the existence of a rough-coated breed of dog in Italy that signalled their discovery of game by assuming a rigid position and placing their bodies in direct line with the find, thus directing the hunter to the hiding place. Although most people are inclined to think of a pointer as a distinct breed of dog, the name actually refers to an entire group of dogs that work the field in a distinctive manner, not unlike that described by the ancient Greeks.

Countries throughout Europe developed their own unique breeds of 'pointer' or 'pointing dog' based upon the demands made by the terrain of their respective locales. The results of these efforts can be seen in such breeds as Germany's Shorthaired Pointer, the Braque Français of France, the breed known simply as the Pointer, which was the

A HUNTER AT HEART

Italian breeders value the hunting ability of the Spinone above any characteristics that are simply 'beauty points.' The appreciation that breeders have historically maintained for their breed's working ability is what has enabled the Spinone to remain one of the Gundog Group's most efficient and tireless field dogs.

UK's contribution, and Italy's Bracco Italiano and Italian Spinone.

The Italian pointers were particularly popular with royalty across Europe in the 14th through 16th centuries. The royal courts rode horseback to the hunt, and good-sized, long-legged dogs suited the occasion well. Controversy exists regarding the root source of the Italian pointing breeds, but one important source of the breed's history is Fiorenzo Fiorone's *The Encyclopaedia of Dogs*, written in collaboration with the Fédération Cynologique Internationale (FCI). The book was first published in Italy as *Enciclopedia del Cane* in 1970. Fiorone's work was closely supervised by Italian breed authorities and is particularly commended by Giulio Colombo, one of the National Association of Italian Dog Fanciers' (NAIDF) most active and highly respected presidents.

BREED NAME

'Spinone' (singular) is pronounced *speh-no-nay*; the plural is spelled 'Spinoni,' not 'Spinone,' and is pronounced *speh-no-nee*.

Fiorone appears to be most closely in agreement with Tschudy's study, which indicates that the Spinone was developed in Italy during the Roman era, with its origins in coarse-haired setters brought there by Greek traders and others from the western Adriatic coast in ancient times. These setters were crossbred with a white Mastiff-type dog already prevalent along the coasts of Italy at the time. The results were called Spinoni.

Accurate representation of the working Spinone appeared in Italian art as early as the 1400s. It should be noted that it was the working ability of the breed that was of primary consequence and what caused the breed to be held in high esteem by Italian sportsmen even then. Paramount concern has been the preservation of these natural abilities. There is no doubt that various strains and deviations existed throughout Italy in the centuries that followed, but there is also fairly unanimous agreement that the dogs also shared many common characteristics.

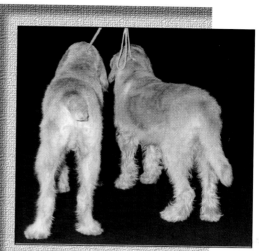

TAIL DOCKING
The tail of the Spinone is docked at birth. Tail docking was performed for many reasons throughout history. Early on, it was thought that the practice prevented a dog from contracting the rabies virus. Another, more plausible, reason was that long tails could easily be injured as the dogs plunged through prickly brush and thicket to perform their duties. This applied to all breeds of dog, but primarily to those whose duties were assisting hunters or herding livestock.

Spinoni with docked (left) and undocked (right) tails.

FAMILY HISTORY
There are breeders in Italy whose families have maintained Spinone lines that trace as far back as the 16th century. These individuals have been highly successful in both hunting and show-ring endeavours.

It appears, even in the initial attempts to define the essence of the Spinone, that certain characteristics were described that have remained constant through the years. Head characteristics, the breed's unique silhouette, the quality of the skin and rough coat texture, along with large size,

continue as the traits necessary to the breed's correct conformation and appearance.

The name of the breed has evolved alongside the development of the breed itself. First called Bracco Spinoso (Prickly Pointer), and Bracco Spinone later, finally in 1887 it was decided to call the breed simply Spinone.

The exact translation of 'Spinone' in English is, in fact, 'very prickly.' Some say the name describes the quality of the coat. Still others believe the name indicates the type of ground upon which the dogs work so efficiently—ground thickly overgrown with every kind of dense prickly bush.

A definitive standard for the breed was written in 1939 by Giuseppe Solaro. This standard remained basically unaltered until 1944 when it was modified by the governing body for all pure-bred dog activities in Italy, Ente Nazionale della Cinofilia Italiano (ENCI).

The two World Wars did little to assist or even maintain the development of the Spinone, but, at the close of World War II, devoted breed fanciers gathered the remaining specimens of the breed and planned careful breedings to eliminate the undesirable qualities contributed by unfortunate crosses to other breeds. Great credit must go to the members of the Italian breed club, La Famiglia dello Spinoni, for the breed's renaissance. Formed in 1950, the organisation was given recognition by the ENCI as the official breed club in Italy. The name of the club has since been changed to Club Italiano Spinoni (CISp).

THE SPINONE IN ENGLAND
There is little doubt but little documentation of the importation of Spinoni into Britain throughout the early years of the 20th century. Attempts to establish the breed, however, went unrewarded. Then, late in the 1950s, the internationally famous concert pianist Semprini brought a pair of Spinoni named Arno and Gita with him when he toured the UK. The pair was housed at Ryslip Kennels from 1957 to 1958 and during that time Gita whelped a litter. The Kennel Club paved the way for future imports to be registered by placing Arno and Gita on the Breed Register.

Over 20 years later, in 1981, Mrs Mary Moore (Odivane) and Ruth Tattersall (Westoy) imported four of the breed into the UK. The imports were a male, Friz del Odivane, and the litter sisters Clara and Megana dei Marchesi dei Galpiott from Odivane. The trio was from Sergio Cantoni's kennel in northern Italy. Dr Tattersall's female named Lidia came from the same kennel. This time interest in the breed flourished. All three of the bitches imported from Sergio Cantoni's kennel were bred, but Megana's

Spinone from the UK, where the breed has only been truly established since the latter half of the 20th century.

Photo circa 1932, published in *Hutchinson's Dog Encyclopaedia.* Part of the caption read: 'Spinone Italiano. Intelligent, intrepid and untiring, this is undoubtedly the most popular with sportsmen in its native country.' The caption also acknowledged the Italian breeders for reviving the breed from near-extinction.

A handsome pair of modern-day Spinone from the UK.

two litters by Friz are those that had the greatest impact and are credited as becoming the corner-stone of the breed in the UK.

The Italian Spinone Club of Great Britain (ISCGB) was organised through the efforts of many breed diehards including Dr Tattersall, Glenys Barlow (Wintercleugh), Cyndy and Malcolm Bevan (Snowlodge), Margaret and John Curgenven (Chruston), Jean Houltram (Caldocani), Viv Rosser (Nantiderri), Lorraine Spencer (Bannonbrig), Gael Stenton (Gaesten) and Helen Thomson (Deldawn).

Initially entered and shown in rare-breed competition, the Spinone made rapid headway with impressive wins in that category as early as 1986 with Best Rare Breed in Show awards. Linda Collins' Sacul Romeo Rio of Wynsett and Rio's granddaughter, Gallowdyke Pawnee, owned by Mike Gadsby and her breeders Sheila and John Piggin, both achieved the Best Rare Breed in Show distinction. Rio was Top-Winning Rare Breed Dog for 1986.

The ISCGB held its first Open Show in 1989. Topping the entry was Mrs Collins' Sacul Romeo Rio of Wynsett, with Best Puppy in

Show being awarded to Mr and Mrs Shimell's Connomar Careena. The year 1994 proved to be a banner year for the breed—the Italian Spinone became eligible to receive Challenge Certificates (CCs). The efforts of the breed's many staunch supporters were finally rewarded.

The first Show Champion was Gallowdyke Wreckless Eric at Sundeala who, after winning his first two CCs at Crufts and the Scottish Kennel Club, acquired the title at ISCGB's first Championship event in June 1994.

Eric was owned by Barbara Davies and Michael Gadsby and bred by John and Sheila Piggin and Michael Gadsby.

Dedicated breed fanciers began to express some concern over the fact that the Spinone, though widely used throughout Europe as a hunting dog, was not receiving the field trial support that the breed warranted in the UK. Thus, a sigh of relief was released when Sh Ch Sentling Zenzero achieved his Gundog Working Certificate at the German Wirehaired Pointer Club's novice

'Mery' was a Best of Breed winner from the early 1930s, a time when the Spinone was a known solely as a working dog and was a rarity in the show ring.

field trial in December 1998. In so doing, Zenzero became Britain's first Champion Italian Spinone. The achievement was particularly noteworthy in that Zenzero, among his many outstanding victories, also claimed first in the Gundog Group at Birmingham National and Best in Show at the breed club Championship Show under judge Penny Robertson. He completed 1998 as the Top-Winning Spinone. Zenzero is regularly worked during the shooting season by his owners, Liz and Jonathan Shaw, who bred him. He was whelped in April 1994 in a litter by Wynsett Jumpin' Jack Flash ex Sentling Ancona. Ancona's litter brother, Italian Sh Ch Sentling Affidato, is the only UK-bred Spinone to win a title in the breed's home country.

Meanwhile, in Italy, the fanciers of the breed have expressed wonder at the fact that the breed is referred to as the Italian Spinone in England. In an article written for *Dog News* by Italian breed authority and judge Dr G W Mentasti, he states, 'To start with, we must define the name of the breed: Spinone, not Italian Spinone. In the FCI list there is only one Spinone, and only one breed with Spinone characteristics. So, there is really no need to add further adjectives.'

Nonetheless, the fact remains that the breed is known

Although still considered a rare breed, Spinoni are becoming more well known world-wide. This quality example hails from the Netherlands.

throughout the UK and in America as the Italian Spinone. It is highly doubtful that any change in the name will occur, as there are many breeds in the UK that are happily burdened by superfluous adjectives (Hungarian Vizsla, Australian Silky Terrier, Japanese Shiba Inu, etc.).

THE SPINONE IN THE UNITED STATES

Ongoing enthusiasm for the many qualities of the Spinone could not help but eventually reach the shores of America. Through the years, a good number of British exports have reached American shores. Long a member of the American Kennel Club's (AKC) Miscellaneous Class, the breed was finally granted full recognition in February 2000 and became eligible to compete for championship status in September 2000.

There is probably nothing quite so captivating as a comical little Spinone puppy with its floppy ears, gangly legs and sweet expression. If you haven't fully decided whether or not to add a Spinone puppy to your life, a visit to the home or kennel where there is a litter of puppies is probably *not* the best idea in the world. Anyone even thinking of dog ownership is going to be hard-pressed to resist these prickly Italian charmers.

For this very reason, the person who anticipates owning a Spinone must give serious thought to the final decision. All puppies are cute and cuddly. Spinone puppies are certainly no exception. Puppies are charming and seductive, but puppies are living, breathing and very adventurous little creatures. Not only that, they depend entirely upon their human owners for everything once they leave their mother and littermates behind.

BEFORE YOU BUY
Careful consideration is appropriate regardless of any breed you might be considering. However, there are special considerations for those who might be thinking about bringing a Spinone puppy into their lives.

The Spinone is a hunting dog. The breed was created to hunt, and centuries have been invested in cultivating and developing the breed's hunting characteristics. The Spinone's mental and physical development depends upon his being given the opportunity to exercise the mental and physical characteristics that he has inherited.

The Spinone needs room to run fast and long and over all kinds of terrain. He must be given opportunity to smell the smells, hear the sounds and see the creatures in nature that will stimulate all of the characteristics that his ancestors have passed down to him. These needs cannot be satisfied by once around the block a few times a week!

If not given these opportunities, the Spinone puppy can become a frustrated adolescent who vents these frustrations in ways that will make you regret ever having considered dog ownership. Is the dog being impossible and incorrigible? No! The dog is simply following his nature, which demands that he put his incomparable energy level to good use.

Failure to think ahead and understand the amount of time and readjustment that dog ownership involves is one of the primary reasons that there are so many abandoned canines that end their lives in animal-rescue centres and shelters. Buying a dog, especially a puppy, before someone is absolutely sure he wants to make that commitment can be a serious mistake.

Before a person decides to buy a dog, there are some very basic conditions that must be considered. One of the first significant questions that must be answered is whether or not the person who will actually be given the responsibility of the dog's care actually wants a dog—particularly a dog that demands the level of outdoor action that the Spinone requires. This may sound like a moot point, but wanting a dog and wanting to care for it properly do not necessarily go hand in hand.

Children are often wildly enthusiastic about having a dog. Parents are often easily persuaded, given that most people recognise that pets are a wonderful method of teaching children responsibility. It should be remembered, however, that childhood enthusiasm can inspire a youngster to promise anything to get what he wants...but that same enthusiasm may wane very quickly. Further, today's children have extremely busy schedules

DOGS, DOGS, GOOD FOR YOUR HEART!

People usually purchase dogs for companionship, but studies show that dogs can help to improve their owners' health and level of activity, as well as lower a human's risk of coronary heart disease. Without even realising it, when a person puts time into exercising, grooming and feeding a dog, he also puts more time into his own personal health care. Dog owners establish more routine schedules for their dogs to follow, which can have positive effects on a human's health. Dogs also teach us patience, offer unconditional love and provide the joy of having a furry friend to pet!

If the Spinone is properly introduced, and the children are instructed in the proper handling of the dog, a wonderful relationship usually develops.

with homework, extra-curricular activities and social events. Who will take care of the puppy once the novelty wears off and, again, does that person want a dog?

Desire to own a dog aside, does the lifestyle of the family actually provide for responsible dog ownership? If the entire family is away from early morning to late at night, who will provide for all of a puppy's needs? Feeding, lots of exercise time, outdoor access and the like cannot be provided if no one is home.

Another important factor to consider is whether or not the breed of dog is suitable for the person or the family with whom it will be living. A fully-grown Spinone can handle the rough-and-tumble play of young children, though a puppy cannot. A very young Spinone puppy should only be allowed playtime with young children when adults are present to supervise. The very young Spinone puppy can be dropped or injured unintention-ally by children unable to properly hold or carry the puppy. On the other hand, the rapidly growing Spinone puppy has no idea of its size or strength and could easily upend and injure a toddler unintentionally.

The grooming of an adult Spinone doesn't require as much time and patience as do the luxuriously coated breeds, but

that does not mean the breed needs no grooming—on the contrary! The owner must commit to keeping the Spinone's coat in good condition, free of mats, tangles, burrs and pesky parasites.

As great as claims are for a Spinone's adaptability and intelli-gence, remember there is no dog, no matter what breed, that doesn't need to be taught every household rule that must be observed. Some dogs learn more quickly than others, and puppies are just as inclined to forget or disregard lessons as are human children.

WHY A PURE-BRED DOG?
It is almost impossible to determine what a mixed-breed puppy will look like as an adult. More importantly, it is impossible to determine what the temperament of a puppy of mixed parentage is going to be like. Will it be suitable for the person or family who wishes to own it? If the puppy grows up to be too big, too hairy or too active for the owner, what then will happen to it?

Size and temperament can vary to a degree, even within pure-bred dogs. Still, controlled breeding over many generations has produced dogs giving us reasonable assurance of what a pure-bred puppy will look and act like when it reaches maturity. This predictability is more important than one might think.

The sweet, pleading expression of the Spinone is one of the breed's most endearing features.

Just about any dog whose background is made up of sound and sane individuals has the potential to be a loving companion. However, the predictability of a pure-bred dog offers reasonable insurance that it will suit not only the person's aesthetic demands but also the owner's lifestyle.

Before you bring a Spinone puppy into your household, visit breeders and spend as much time with both puppies and adults as you can. You must confirm that the adult Spinone is the dog that appeals to you aesthetically and temperamentally, and above all be certain that you will in fact be a suitable owner for the breed.

CHARACTER OF THE SPINONE

The Spinone—puppy or adult—has the sweetest, most beguiling expression that you can find on any breed of dog. Thus, it is all the more surprising to find the lengths to which the Spinone will go to accomplish his ends—particularly so if those ends involve food! A Spinone is always hungry—morning, noon and night. The fact that he's just had his dinner is no deterrent. If food exists, your Spinone wants it! Spinoni are clever to a fault and can work out ways to get into and out of any cupboard or enclosure that would be entirely foolproof to most other breeds—even if it means eating through what stands between him and the snack he's after.

Immediately after food on the Spinone's list of favourite things, or perhaps even right alongside of it, is the breed's love of the outdoors and being put to work in the capacity for which the breed was created—hunting! And when speaking of hunting, it cannot be

FAMILY DEVOTION

There is no doubt that the trait endearing the Spinone to the many families that own the breed is its devotion to the entire family. This is particularly so in regard to the children of the family. Even well-behaved toddlers find the adult Spinone to be a willing and patient playmate who can even be relied upon to invent games if need be to keep a child amused.

stressed enough that a Spinone is first and foremost a hunting dog. Are there Spinoni that are bred just to be pets? Not by people who truly love the breed!

The desire and the ability to hunt are what have allowed the Spinone to flourish throughout its history. Most Spinone show dogs are father's 'hunting chum' on Saturday and mum and the children's show dog on Sunday. People who love the Spinone would have it no other way.

Spinoni are listed among the most intelligent of all the breeds, a distinction that is both good and bad—good in that they can learn just about anything you want to teach them, but bad in that a Spinone can become bored very easily without activities that keep him mentally and physically busy.

The Spinone is not a breed that can be left on its own continuously or kept outdoors without another canine companion. The breed's long-standing history working alongside man and other dogs in the field has made the Spinone a very social creature. Denied the opportunity to be with those he loves, the Spinone will demand attention by developing behavioural problems. Destructive digging, chewing and barking are usually signs of a bored Spinone.

The Spinone is an ideal family dog in that he is able to share his devotion with every member of the family and has an innate ability to adjust his own mood to that to that of the family member he is with. He will sound the alarm to alert the family to the approach of a stranger, but will be delighted to greet that same stranger if given assurance that all is well.

Even the ever-active Spinone needs to take a break from time to time!

TRAINABILITY OF THE BREED

Life is indeed the proverbial 'bowl of cherries' to the Spinone, and, admittedly, the young dog may appear to be more than just a bit silly. However, do not mistake these characteristics for stupidity. On the contrary, this is an extremely clever breed that is prone to study your every action and reaction. Should you not establish the fact that you indeed are the pack leader early on, expect your Spinone to try his hand at it! By and large, the breed is most amiable and there is no reason for the breed to be anything else unless you provide the circumstances.

There are times when your Spinone needs correction, and you must be forthright and uncompromising in this respect. This, however, never means striking your dog. A rap on the nose with a finger or holding his head in your hands with eye-to-eye contact and a stern 'No!' may be necessary and will not shatter the Spinone, but

> **SIZE DIFFERENCES**
> Both the male and female Spinoni make excellent companions and work equally well in the field. Their primary difference is in height and weight. Recommended size for males is 60–70 cms (23.5–27.5 ins) and 34–39 kgs (76–85 lbs). Females should be between 59–65 cms (23–25.5 ins) and 29–34 kgs (64–75 lbs).

harsh methods can destroy the dog's spirit and trainability.

Repetition and determination work best with the breed, and, once learned, lessons seem almost a natural part of the Spinone's character. Avoidance of bad habits works best. Not allowing unwanted behaviour to occur in the first place is infinitely simpler than trying to convince your Spinone pup to stop something he has been doing right along.

Those who work with the Spinone in the field are quick to say that, once trained, the Spinone does not forget. He is a ready and willing hunter who is happy to work almost any terrain from the mountains to pond but, at his very best, penetrating dense growth and underbrush. The working Spinone has great endurance and tolerance for both heat and cold. He maintains excellent contact skills while working and is a prompt and dependable retriever.

A Spinone likes to keep busy...and if not otherwise occupied, you can be sure he'll find something to do!

SPINONI AND THE WORLD AT LARGE

Spinoni love their own people and their normally happy-go-lucky manner belies a protective instinct that emerges when something unusual occurs. This he handles by sounding the alarm—barking. Some Spinoni become completely enthralled with the sound of their own voices and entertain themselves by barking for no other reason than they enjoy it. Not a good idea unless you and your Spinone live in some remote part of a forest!

Although you undoubtedly will want to be forewarned with the arrival of a stranger, the warning doesn't have to continue *ad infinitum*. After a few barks, praise and pet your dog. This will usually make him pause—briefly. Once he attempts to begin barking again, like most any Spinone will, say 'No!' immediately. It will take some persistence on your part, but eventually you will get your message through.

OTHER PETS AND ANIMALS

Some Spinoni are a bit reserved when strange dogs approach, others know no enemies in the canine world. Most properly raised Spinoni are happy to co-exist with any other four-legged family pet that might share the home. Winged pets and rodents will have little problem with a Spinone as long as they are

COLOURS

Although one is more apt to see a predominance of white and orange Spinoni at dog shows, the breed is found in brown roan coloration as well. Both colours are equally acceptable according to the breed standard and in the show ring. Preference is strictly on the part of the beholder.

confined to their cages. Everything in a Spinone's genetic makeup tells the dog something must be done about these little critters when they are loose. It will take a good deal of restraint for a Spinone to remain calm and indifferent with the family budgerigar or chipmunk darting about the room.

All hunting dogs have the chase instinct, and if your cat or resident dog will be inclined to bolt at the sight of this new intruder, it is best to keep your Spinone on his leash. If the relationship begins with the chase, it will take a lot of doing to break the resident animal's hasty retreat and your Spinone's

DO YOU KNOW ABOUT HIP DYSPLASIA?

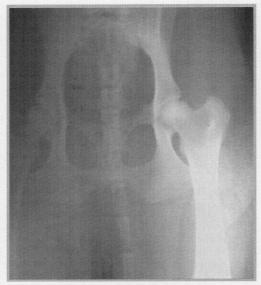

X-ray of a dog with 'Good' hips.

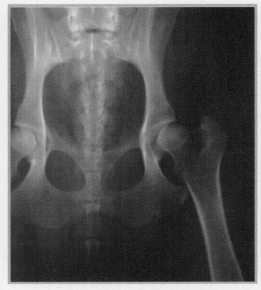

X-ray of a dog with 'Moderate' dysplastic hips.

Hip dysplasia is a fairly common condition found in pure-bred dogs. When a dog has hip dysplasia, its hind leg has an incorrectly formed hip joint. By constant use of the hip joint, it becomes more and more loose, wears abnormally and may become arthritic.

Hip dysplasia can only be confirmed with an x-ray, but certain symptoms may indicate a problem. Your dog may have a hip dysplasia problem if it walks in a peculiar manner, hops instead of smoothly runs, uses its hind legs in unison (to keep the pressure off the weak joint), has trouble getting up from a prone position or always sits with both legs together on one side of its body.

As the dog matures, it may adapt well to life with a bad hip, but in a few years the arthritis develops and many dogs with hip dysplasia become cripples.

Hip dysplasia is considered an inherited disease and only can be diagnosed definitively when the dog is two years old. Some experts claim that a special diet might help your puppy outgrow the bad hip, but the usual treatments are surgical. The removal of the pectineus muscle, the removal of the round part of the femur, reconstructing the pelvis and replacing the hip with an artificial one are all surgical interventions that are expensive, but they are usually very successful. Follow the advice of your veterinary surgeon.

willingness to pursue. Give them time to become acquainted and trust each other before they are free to interact on their own.

HEALTH CONCERNS
It is not the least bit unusual to have the well-bred and well-cared-for Spinone live to be 12 years old, and there are many cases of individuals living to be 14 years of age and in relatively good health. Since your Spinone puppy will be living with you for many, many years, you want those years to be enjoyable ones in which your dog leads a happy, healthy life. Like all breeds of dogs, there are problems in the Spinone breed that conscientious breeders strive to avoid through screening and rigid selection of breeding stock.

CANINE CEREBELLAR ATAXIA (CCA)
Research indicates that cerebellar ataxia is an heritable disease of the cerebellum, the part of the brain that controls a dog's gait. Affected dogs have a poorly controlled or wobbly gait, and these symptoms have been all found in young dogs. Studies have confirmed that the disease is caused by a simple recessive gene. Strict controls in the selection of breeding stock are necessary in order to rid lines of the problem and to prevent the disease from being transmitted further.

HIP DYSPLASIA
Hip dysplasia is a developmental disease of the hip joint. The result is instability of the hip joint due to abnormal contours of one or both of the hip joints. Affected dogs might show tenderness in the hip, walk with a limp or swaying gait or experience difficulty when getting up after sleeping. Hip dysplasia first

ADOPTING AN ADULT
Adopting an adult Spinone can be a good choice for an adult or elderly person who wishes to avoid the trials of puppyhood. It should be understood that, like any adult, the mature Spinone may have developed behaviours not suitable for the new household. Therefore, bringing a mature Spinone into the home should always be done on a trial basis.

KEEP YOUR ITALIAN SPINONE BUSY

A bored Spinone is a chewing Spinone. Sufficient exercise helps keep that high energy level in check and is the best deterrent for chewing. In preparation for field work, the puppy can be introduced to a game bird wing. Watching this meeting awaken the innate hunting instinct that lies just below the surface of every Spinone's consciousness can be a delight for both dog and owner.

exhibits suspicious symptoms should be x-rayed and the problem discussed with both the breeder from whom you purchased your dog and your veterinary surgeon.

BLOAT

Although bloat (gastric torsion) is not actually known to be an inherited problem, it does occur in deep-chested breeds such as the Spinone. Little is known about the actual cause of bloat. Many theories have been offered but none actually proven. This often-fatal condition seems to occur frequently at night after the dog has had a large meal, has ingested a great deal of water and then exercises strenuously. Symptoms can range from a severe attack of gas to death. It can occur so suddenly and swiftly

A good way to keep the Spinone busy is to get him wet! Although not a water dog by nature, many excel at water retrieving and enjoy a good swim.

appears during growing stages and usually becomes progressively worse as the dog grows older. Controversy surrounds this disease regarding its genetic basis. It is now believed that, while propensity for the condition can be inherited, it is yet another condition that can be promoted by improper feeding and over-supplementation in puppies and young dogs as well as by environmental factors.

Surgery to replace affected hips has been developed. All breeding stock and any dog that

that only immediate attention by a vet experienced in dealing with the condition will save your dog's life.

Simply described, bloat causes the stomach to twist so that both ends are closed off. The food contained in the stomach ferments but gasses cannot escape, thereby causing the stomach to swell greatly pressuring the entire diaphragm and consequently leading to extreme cardiac and respiratory complications. The affected dog is in extreme pain and death can follow very quickly unless the gas is released through surgery.

EYE PROBLEMS

The Spinone's loose skin can create a number of problems manifesting themselves in and surrounding the eye. Entropion and ectropion in puppies and adolescents can be temporary, lasting only until maturity is reached and full size is achieved, taking up the loose skin. These conditions can persist into adulthood and may require veterinary assistance including surgery in some cases.

Entropion is an anatomical abnormality due to spasm and contraction of the muscles controlling the eye rims. This causes the affected eyelids to turn and roll in towards the eyeball. The resulting contact of eyelash to eyeball produces a state of semi-

HOW TO PREVENT BLOAT

Research has confirmed that the structure of deep-chested breeds contributes to their predisposition to bloat. Nevertheless, there are several precautions that you can take to reduce the risk of this condition:

• Feed your dog twice daily rather than offer one big meal.
• Do not exercise your dog for at least one hour before and two hours after he has eaten.
• Make certain that your dog is calm and not overly excited while he is eating. It has been proven that nervous or overly excited dogs are more prone to develop bloat.
• Add a small portion of moist meat product to his dried food ration.
• Serve his meals in an elevated bowl stand, which avoids the dog's craning his neck while eating.
• To prevent your dog from gobbling his food too quickly, and thereby swallowing air, put some large (unswallowable) toys into his bowl so that he will have to eat around them to get his food.

permanent irritation and possible permanent damage to the eyeball itself. Usually it is the lower lid that is affected but the upper lid may be affected as well. Ectropion is the scientific term for exceedingly loose lower eyelids causing inflammation of the exposed areas of the eye and tear overflow.

INTRODUCTION TO THE STANDARD

In the earliest days of man's relationship with dogs, he began to see that those particular dogs constructed in a certain way were more successful at performing the tasks assigned to them. It then became those particular charac-teristics that guided man's breeding practices. The people who kept the dogs that were serving them best gathered to make comparisons and seek out stock to improve their own dogs. The more successful keepers were asked to observe the dogs at work and evaluate them.

With industrialisation, little villages grew into large cities and towns and the citizenry moved into urban dwellings. Fewer and fewer dogs were given the opportunity to perform in the capacity for which their breeds were created. To avoid the respec-tive breeds' losing their ability to perform, dog fanciers began to select their stock on the basis of the conformation that they determined would produce the most successful workers. The guidelines, or 'standards,' became theoretical rather than practical. It should be noted here that these

descriptions were the forerunners of what are known as 'breed standards' today and that they were written by knowledgeable individuals in the breed for their peers. The descriptions were used primarily as checklists or 'blueprints' to breed by and they served as reminders so that important points of conformation would not be lost.

In many cases, the accent that had previously been on function was now placed on form. It should be easy to see, once form was the keynote, how breeds whose only purpose was to be aesthetically pleasing would gain an equal place of respect alongside their working relatives. It should be understood, however, that not all fanciers neglected the original purpose of their breeds. For example, in Italy, devotees of the Spinone jealously have guarded the breed's hunting ability through the centuries and have been adamant in maintaining the characteristics that enable their breed to excel in this capacity.

Today's Spinone standard describes the ideal hunting dog. It is based upon the original standard drafted in Italy that was written by individuals versed in the breed's type and ability in the field. It includes a description of ideal structure, temperament, coat, colour and gait (the manner in which the breed moves). All of these descriptions are based upon what constitutes an efficient hunter and reliable companion.

As stated, breed standards are used by breeders to assist them in breeding toward their goal of perfection. While no dog is absolutely perfect, the dogs that adhere most closely to the ideal are what breeders will determine to be show or breeding stock, and the dogs that deviate to any great extent are considered companion or pet stock. The standard is also used by dog show judges to compare actual dogs to the ideal. The dog adhering most closely to this ideal is the winner of its class, and so on down the line.

THE KENNEL CLUB STANDARD FOR THE ITALIAN SPINONE

General Appearance: Solid, squarely built, strong bone and well muscled. Kind and earnest expression.

Characteristics: Intrepid and untiring, very hardy, adaptable to any terrain including water. All-purpose gundog.

Temperament: Faithful, intelligent, patient and affectionate.

Head and Skull: Head long, skull flat, lean; sides gently sloping and very slightly rounded, equal in length from well developed occiput to stop as from gently sloping stop to tip of nose. Median furrow pronounced. Nose large, spongy in appearance, protruding over rather thin lips.

THE IDEAL SPECIMEN

According to The Kennel Club, 'The Breed Standard is the "Blueprint" of the ideal specimen in each breed approved by a governing body, e.g. The Kennel Club, the Fédération Cynologique Internationale (FCI) and the American Kennel Club.

The Kennel Club writes and revises Breed Standards taking account of the advice of Breed Councils/Clubs. Breed Standards are not changed lightly to avoid "changing the standard to fit the current dogs" and the health and well-being of future dogs is always taken into account when new standards are prepared or existing ones altered.'

Eyes: Large, fairly round and open, eyelids close fitting. Deep yellow in white, and white and orange; ochre in brown roans.

Ears: Set on level with corner of eye, long, but not more than 5 cms (2 ins) below jaw line, pendulous, forward edge touching cheek. Triangular in shape, slightly rounded at tip, covered with thick short hair, longer and denser at edges.

Mouth: Jaws powerful with a perfect, regular and complete scissor bite, i.e. upper teeth closely overlapping lower teeth and set square to the jaws. Lips rather thin.

Neck: Strong, muscular, fairly short, merging into shoulder, slight, divided dewlap.

Forequarters: Shoulders strong, well muscled and well laid back. Points of shoulder set well apart. Forelegs straight, bone oval; strong, well defined tendons. Pasterns slightly sloping when

Correct structure is of utmost importance, especially in a breed whose construction enables it to perform its intended duty. In the show ring, the judge feels to make sure that correct bone structure is present.

> **BREEDER'S BLUEPRINT**
> If you are considering breeding your bitch, it is very important that you are familiar with the breed standard. Reputable breeders breed with the intention of producing dogs that are as close as possible to the standard and that contribute to the advancement of the breed. Study the standard for both physical appearance and temperament, and make certain your bitch and your chosen stud dog measure up.

viewed from side, elbows turning neither in nor out.

Body: Length equal to height at withers, chest broad, open, well let down. Brisket reaching at least to level of elbows. Front of sternum comes well forward below points of shoulders. Ribs open, well sprung. Topline, a very slight slope from raised withers to well muscled loins, slight rise from loin to broad and muscular croup, croup sloping.

Hindquarters: Thighs long, broad, muscular and strong. Hocks well let down. Metatarsals vertical on extension of buttock line. Tendons clearly visible.

Feet: Front compact, round. Hindfeet slightly oval. Toes arched, covered with short thick hair especially between toes. Nails

An artist's sketch of the correct Spinone head.

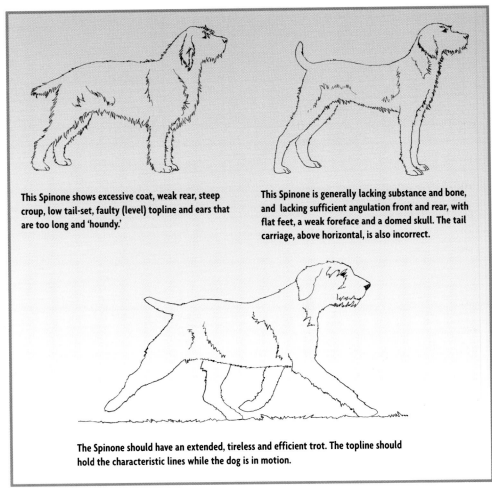

This Spinone shows excessive coat, weak rear, steep croup, low tail-set, faulty (level) topline and ears that are too long and 'houndy.'

This Spinone is generally lacking substance and bone, and lacking sufficient angulation front and rear, with flat feet, a weak foreface and a domed skull. The tail carriage, above horizontal, is also incorrect.

The Spinone should have an extended, tireless and efficient trot. The topline should hold the characteristic lines while the dog is in motion.

strong, arched. Pads hard. Pigmented according to coat colours. Never black. Dewclaws on all four feet.

Tail: Thick at base, set on as a continuation of croup line, carried horizontally or down, customarily docked to half its length.

Gait/Movement: Free, relaxed and capable of fast trot.

Coat: Tough, thick, slightly wiry, close fitting, length 4–6 cms (1.5–2.5 ins) on body, shorter on nasal bridge, ears and head, even shorter on front of legs and feet. Eyebrows consist of longer stiffer hair; even longer but softer hair covers cheeks and upper lips forming moustache and beard. Skin thick and leathery.

Colour: White, white with orange markings; solid white peppered orange, white with brown markings, white speckled with brown (brown roan), with or without large brown markings. Pigment of skin, eyelids, nose, lips and pads fleshy red in white dogs, deeper in white/orange and brown roan dogs.

Size: Height: dogs: 60–70 cms (23.5–27.5 ins); bitches: 59–65 cms (23–25.5 ins). Weight: dogs 34–39 kgs (75–86 lbs); bitches: 29–34 kgs (64–75 lbs).

Faults: Any departure from the foregoing points should be considered a fault and the seriousness with which the fault should be regarded should be in exact proportion to its degree.

Note: Male animals should have two apparently normal testicles fully descended into the scrotum.

While hard to predict show quality in young pups, quality pups come from quality breeding. Breeders have knowledge of their own lines and should have an idea of how their pups will develop.

ITALIAN SPINONE

HOW TO SELECT A SPINONE BREEDER AND PUPPY

Your Spinone should only be purchased from a breeder who has earned a reputation for consistently producing dogs that are mentally and physically sound. The only way a breeder can earn this reputation is through selective breeding aimed at eliminating genetic weaknesses.

The first question a prospective owner should ask a Spinone breeder is, 'What do you do with your dogs?' Does he hunt his dogs or compete in field trials? Are the dogs shown in conformation competition, obedience, etc? If the person with whom you are talking breeds Spinoni only to sell pet puppies, go somewhere else for your dog!

Cleanliness in both the dogs and the areas in which the dogs are kept is a bottom-line requirement, so take note of this when you visit the facility. This is the first clue that tells you how much the breeder cares about the dogs he owns.

The Spinone puppy you buy should be a happy and bouncy extrovert. However, you need not necessarily select the leader of the little pack. The extremely bold and

extroverted pup will undoubtedly demand a lot more exercise and attention to keep him wound down than will his calmer, content littermates. This does not mean you should select a shy, shrinking-violet puppy. This, of course, is not typical of correct Spinone attitude.

Healthy Spinone puppies are strong and firm to the touch, never

You can learn quite a bit about the puppies' future temperament by observing them at play with their parents and littermates.

PUPPY SELECTION

Your selection of a good puppy can be determined by your needs. A show potential or a good pet? It is your choice. Every puppy, however, should be of good temperament. Although show-quality puppies are bred and raised with emphasis on physical conformation, responsible breeders strive for equally good temperament. Do not buy from a breeder who concentrates solely on physical beauty at the expense of personality and work ability.

bony or, on the other hand, obese and bloated. Coats will be lustrous with no sign of dry or flaky skin. The inside of the puppy's ears should be pink and clean. Dark discharge or a bad odour could indicate ear mites, a sure sign of poor maintenance. The healthy Spinone puppy's breath smells sweet. The teeth are clean and

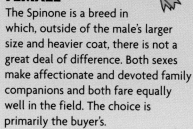

SELECTING MALE OR FEMALE

The Spinone is a breed in which, outside of the male's larger size and heavier coat, there is not a great deal of difference. Both sexes make affectionate and devoted family companions and both fare equally well in the field. The choice is primarily the buyer's.

Females do have their semi-annual heat cycles once they have passed nine or ten months of age. A watchful eye is necessary at this time to avoid unwanted puppies' being sired by some marauding male.

In some instances, teaching males not to 'lift their legs' and urinate indoors can present a problem, but most Spinone males are not difficult to correct in this respect. Spinone males can get 'wanderlust' if not kept active and interested at home—particularly if the female Dachshund or Cocker Spaniel up the hill is having her heat period. Nearly all sexually related problems can be avoided by having the pet Spinone 'altered.' Spaying the female and neutering the male save the pet owner all the headaches of either of the sexually related problems without changing the character of the breed.

If you have decided upon the sex of the puppy you want, stand by your choice and do not have someone change your mind because that is 'all that is left.'

white, and there should never be any malformation of the mouth or jaw. The puppy's eyes should be clear and bright. Eyes that appear runny and irritated indicate serious problems. There should be no sign of discharge from the nose nor should it ever be crusted or runny. Coughing and diarrhoea are danger signals as are any eruptions on the skin.

The healthy Spinone puppy's front legs should be straight as little posts. Even at an early age, a Spinone puppy's legs appear long in proportion and give the youngster a somewhat awkward gangly look. Yet, movement is true and there should be no hint of lameness or difficulty when moving.

If the prospective owner is considering a show career for his puppy, he should be aware that the most any breeder can offer is an opinion on the 'show potential' of a particular puppy. Any predictions that breeders make about a puppy's future should be based upon their experience with past litters that have produced winning show dogs. It is obvious that the more successful a breeder has been in producing winning Spinoni over the years, the broader his or her base of comparison will be. Give serious consideration to both what the standard says a show-type Spinone must look like and to what the breeder's recommendations are.

PREPARING FOR PUP
Unfortunately, when a puppy is bought by someone who does not take into consideration the time and attention that dog ownership requires, it is the puppy who suffers when he is either abandoned or placed in a shelter by a frustrated owner. So all of the 'homework' you do in preparation for your pup's arrival will benefit you both. The more informed you are, the more you will know what to expect and the better equipped you will be to handle the ups and downs of raising a puppy. Hopefully, everyone in the household is willing to do his part in raising and caring for the pup. The anticipation of owning a dog often brings a lot of promises from excited family members: 'I will walk him every day,' 'I will feed him,' 'I will house-train him,' etc., but these things take time and effort, and promises can easily be forgotten once the novelty of the new pet has worn off.

Welcoming your new Spinone pup home is an exciting and joyful occasion!

PUPPY APPEARANCE
Your puppy should have a well-fed appearance but not a distended abdomen, which may indicate worms or incorrect feeding, or both. The body should be firm, with a solid feel. The skin of the abdomen should be pale pink and clean, without signs of scratching or rash.

COMMITMENT OF OWNERSHIP

After considering all of these factors, you have most likely already made some very important decisions about selecting your puppy. You have chosen a Spinone, which means that you have decided which characteristics you want in a dog and what type of dog will best fit into your family and lifestyle. If you have selected a breeder, you have gone a step further—you have done your research and found a responsible, conscientious person who breeds quality Spinoni and who should be a reliable source of help as you and your puppy adjust to life together. If you have observed a litter in action, you have obtained a firsthand look at the dynamics of a puppy 'pack' and, thus, you have learned about each pup's individual personality—perhaps you have even found one that particularly appeals to you.

However, even if you have not yet found the Spinone puppy of your dreams, observing pups will help you learn to recognise certain behaviour and to determine what a pup's behaviour indicates about his temperament. You will be able to pick out which pups are the leaders, which ones are less outgoing, which ones are confident, which ones are shy, playful, friendly, aggressive, etc. Equally as important, you will learn to recognise what a healthy pup should look and act

DID YOU KNOW?
You should not even think about buying a puppy that looks sick, undernourished, overly frightened or nervous. Sometimes a timid puppy will warm up to you after a 30-minute 'let's-get-acquainted' session.

member of your family. You will come to realise that, while buying a puppy is a pleasurable and exciting endeavour, it is not something to be taken lightly. Relax...the fun will start when the pup comes home!

PUPPY PERSONALITY
When a litter becomes available to you, choosing a pup out of all those adorable faces will not be an easy task! Sound temperament is of utmost importance, but each pup has its own personality and some may be better suited to you than others. A feisty, independent pup will do well in a home with older children and adults, while quiet, shy puppies will thrive in a home with minimal noise and distractions. Your breeder knows the pups best and should be able to guide you in the right direction.

like. All of these things will help you in your search, and when you find the Spinone that was meant for you, you will know it!

Researching your breed, selecting a responsible breeder and observing as many pups as possible are all important steps on the way to dog ownership. It may seem like a lot of effort...and you have not even taken the pup home yet! Remember, though, you cannot be too careful when it comes to deciding on the type of dog you want and finding out about your prospective pup's background. Buying a puppy is not—or should not be—just another whimsical purchase. This is one instance in which you actually do get to choose your own family! You may be thinking that buying a puppy should be fun— it should not be so serious and so much work. Keep in mind that your puppy is not a cuddly stuffed toy or decorative lawn ornament; rather, he is a living creature that will become a real

Always keep in mind that a puppy is nothing more than a baby in a furry disguise...a baby who is virtually helpless in a human world and who trusts his owner for fulfilment of his basic needs for survival. In addition to food, water and shelter, your pup needs care, protection, guidance

'YOU BETTER SHOP AROUND!'

Finding a reputable breeder that sells healthy pups is very important, but make sure that the breeder you choose is not only someone you respect but also with whom you feel comfortable. Your breeder will be a resource long after you buy your puppy, and you must be able to call with reasonable questions without being made to feel like a pest! If you don't connect on a personal level, investigate some other breeders before making a final decision.

DOCUMENTATION

Two important documents you will get from the breeder are the pup's pedigree and registration certificate. The breeder should register the litter and each pup with The Kennel Club, and it is necessary for you to have the paperwork if you plan on showing or breeding in the future.

Make sure you know the breeder's intentions on which type of registration he will obtain for the pup. There are limited registrations which may prohibit the dog from being shown, being bred or competing in non-conformation trials such as Working or Agility if the breeder feels that the pup is not of sufficient quality to do so. There is also a type of registration that will permit the dog in non-conformation competition only.

On the reverse side of the registration certificate, the new owner can find the transfer section, which must be signed by the breeder.

and love. If you are not prepared to commit to this, then you are not prepared to own a dog.

Wait a minute, you say. How hard could this be? All of my neighbours own dogs and they seem to be doing just fine. Why should I have to worry about all of this? Well, you should not worry about it; in fact, you will probably find that once your Spinone pup gets used to his new home, he will fall into his place in the family quite naturally. However, it never hurts to emphasise the commitment of dog ownership. With some time and patience, it is really not too difficult to raise a curious and exuberant Spinone pup to be a well-adjusted and well-mannered adult dog—a dog that could be your most loyal friend.

PREPARING PUPPY'S PLACE IN YOUR HOME

Researching your breed and finding a breeder are only two aspects of the 'homework' you will have to do before taking your Spinone puppy home. You will also have to prepare your home

DID YOU KNOW?
Breeders rarely release puppies until they are eight to ten weeks of age. This is an acceptable age for most breeds of dog, excepting toy breeds, which are not released until around 12 weeks, given their petite sizes. If a breeder has a puppy that is 12 weeks of age or older, it is likely well socialised and house-trained. Be sure that it is otherwise healthy before deciding to take it home.

INSURANCE
Many good breeders will offer you insurance with your new puppy, which is an excellent idea. The first few weeks of insurance will probably be covered free of charge or with only minimal cost, allowing you to take up the policy when this expires. If you own a pet dog, it is sensible to take out such a policy as veterinary fees can be high, although routine vaccinations and boosters are not covered. Look carefully at the many options open to you before deciding which suits you best.

and family for the new addition. Much as you would prepare a nursery for a newborn baby, you will need to designate a place in your home that will be the puppy's own. How you prepare your home will depend on how much freedom the dog will be allowed. Whatever you decide, you must ensure that he has a place that he can 'call his own.'

When you bring your new puppy into your home, you are

Select a sturdy crate for your Spinone, in a size that will accommodate him when fully grown.

PHOTO COURTESY OF DOSKOCIL

place in your home for the puppy, you are making him feel as welcome as possible in a strange new place. It should not take him long to get used to it, but the sudden shock of being transplanted is somewhat traumatic for a young pup. Imagine how a small child would feel in the same situation—that is how your puppy must be feeling. It is up to you to reassure him and to let him know, 'Little chap, you are going to like it here!'

bringing him into what will become his home as well. Obviously, you did not buy a puppy with the intentions of catering to his every whim and allowing him to 'rule the roost,' but in order for a puppy to grow into a stable, well-adjusted dog, he has to feel comfortable in his surroundings. Remember, he is leaving the warmth and security of his mother and littermates, as well as the familiarity of the only place he has ever known, so it is important to make his transition as easy as possible. By preparing a

CRATE TRAINING TIPS

During crate training, you should partition off the section of the crate in which the pup stays. If he is given too big an area, this will hinder your training efforts. Crate training is based on the fact that a dog does not like to soil his sleeping quarters, so it is ineffective to keep a pup in a crate that is so big that he can eliminate in one end and get far enough away from it to sleep. Also, you want to make the crate den-like for the pup. Blankets and a favourite toy will make the crate cosy for the small pup; as he grows, you may want to evict some of his 'roommates' to make more room.

It will take some coaxing at first, but be patient. Given some time to get used to it, your pup will adapt to his new home-within-a-home quite nicely.

WHAT YOU SHOULD BUY

CRATE

To someone unfamiliar with the use of crates in dog training, it may seem like punishment to shut a dog in a crate, but this is not the case at all. Although all breeders do not advocate crate training, more and more breeders and trainers are recommending crates as preferred tools for show puppies as well as pet puppies. Crates are not cruel—crates have many humane and highly effective uses in dog care and training. For example, crate training is a popular and successful house-training method. In addition, a crate can keep your dog safe during travel and, perhaps most importantly, a crate provides your dog with a place of his own in your home. It serves as a 'doggie bedroom' of sorts—your Spinone can curl up in his crate when he wants to sleep or when he just needs a break. Many dogs sleep in their crates overnight. With soft bedding and his favourite toy, a crate becomes a cosy pseudo-den for your dog. Like his ancestors, he too will seek out the comfort and retreat of a den—you just happen to be providing him with something a little more luxurious than what his early ancestors enjoyed.

As far as purchasing a crate, the type that you buy is up to you. It will most likely be one of the

---

INHERIT THE MIND

In order to know whether or not a puppy will fit into your lifestyle, you need to assess his personality. A good way to do this is to interact with his parents. Your pup inherits not only his appearance but also his personality and temperament from the sire and dam. If the parents are fearful or overly aggressive, these same traits may likely show up in your puppy.

---

two most popular types: wire or fibreglass. There are advantages and disadvantages to each type. For example, a wire crate is more open, allowing the air to flow through and affording the dog a view of what is going on around him, while a fibreglass crate is sturdier. Both can double as travel crates, providing protection for the dog. The size of the crate is another thing to consider. Puppies do not stay puppies forever—in fact, sometimes it seems as if they

Your new Spinone will be part of the family in no time!

Playing and chewing: two activities that Spinone pups like best!! Who will win this friendly game of tug-of-war?

YOUR SCHEDULE . . .
If you lead an erratic, unpredictable life, with daily or weekly changes in your work requirements, consider the problems of owning a puppy. The new puppy has to be fed regularly, socialised (loved, petted, handled, introduced to other people) and, most importantly, allowed to visit outdoors for toilet training. As the dog gets older, it can be more tolerant of deviations in its feeding and toilet relief.

grow right before your eyes. A very small crate may be fine for a very young Spinone pup, but it will not do him much good for long! Unless you have the money and the inclination to buy a new crate every time your pup has a growth spurt, it is better to get one that will accommodate your dog both as a pup and at full size. The extra-large size suits the Spinone best: approximately 68.5 cms (27 ins) wide x 101.5 cms (40 ins) deep x 76 cms (30 ins) high. This size will accommodate through adulthood for even the up-to-standard-sized male.

BEDDING

Veterinary bedding in the dog's crate will help the dog feel more at home, and you may also like to pop in a small blanket. First, this will take the place of the leaves, twigs, etc., that the pup would use in the wild to make a den; the pup can make his own 'burrow' in the crate. Although your pup is

far removed from his den-making ancestors, the denning instinct is still a part of his genetic makeup. Second, until you take your pup home, he has been sleeping amid the warmth of his mother and littermates, and while a blanket is not the same as a warm, breathing body, it still provides heat and something with which to snuggle. You will want to wash your pup's bedding frequently in case he has

MENTAL AND DENTAL
Toys not only help your puppy get the physical and mental stimulation he needs but also provide a great way to keep his teeth clean. Hard rubber or nylon toys, especially those constructed with grooves, are designed to scrape away plaque, preventing bad breath and gum infection.

a toileting 'accident' in his crate, and replace or remove any blanket that becomes ragged and starts to fall apart.

Toys

Toys are a must for dogs of all ages, especially for curious playful pups. Puppies are the 'children' of the dog world, and what child does not love toys? Chew toys provide enjoyment for both dog and owner—your dog will enjoy playing with his favourite toys, while you will enjoy the fact that they distract him from chewing on your expensive shoes and leather sofa. Puppies love to chew; in fact, chewing is a physical need for pups as they are teething, and everything looks appetising! The full range of your possessions— from old tea towel to Oriental carpet—are fair game in the eyes of a teething pup. Puppies are not all that discerning when it comes to finding something literally to 'sink their teeth into'—everything tastes great!

Spinone puppies are fairly aggressive chewers and only the hardest, strongest toys should be offered to them. Breeders advise owners to resist stuffed toys, because they can become de-stuffed in no time. The overly excited pup may ingest the stuffing, which is neither digestible nor nutritious.

Similarly, squeaky toys are

TOYS, TOYS, TOYS!
With a big variety of dog toys available, and so many that look like they would be a lot of fun for a dog, be careful in your selection. It is amazing what a set of puppy teeth can do to an innocent-looking toy, so, obviously, safety is a major consideration. Be sure to choose the most durable products that you can find. Hard nylon bones and toys are a safe bet, and many of them are offered in different scents and flavours that will be sure to capture your dog's attention. It is always fun to play a game of catch with your dog, and there are balls and flying discs that are specially made to withstand dog teeth.

quite popular, but must be avoided for the Spinone. Perhaps a squeaky toy can be used as an aid in training, but not for free play. If a pup 'disembowels' one of these, the small plastic squeaker inside can be dangerous if swallowed. Monitor the condition of all your pup's toys carefully and get rid of any that have been chewed to the point of becoming potentially dangerous.

Be careful of natural bones, which have a tendency to splinter into sharp, dangerous pieces. Also be careful of rawhide, which can turn into pieces that are easy to swallow and become a mushy mess on your carpet.

The retrieving dummy is a favourite for the Spinone. A natural retriever, the Spinone enjoys games of fetch and retrieving practice.

PLAY'S THE THING

Teaching the puppy to play with his toys in running and fetching games is an ideal way to help the puppy develop muscle, learn motor skills and bond with you, his owner and master.

He also needs to learn how to inhibit his bite reflex and never to use his teeth on people, forbidden objects and other animals in play. Whenever you play with your puppy, you make the rules. This becomes an important message to your puppy in teaching him that you are the pack leader and control everything he does in life. Once your dog accepts you as his leader, your relationship with him will be cemented for life.

Your local pet shop will have a wide variety of leads from which you can select a suitable lead for your Spinone.

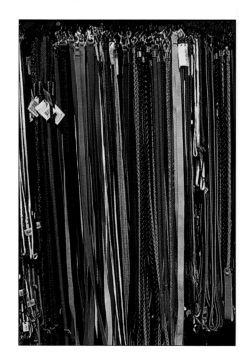

The collar should fit the dog securely and comfortably.

LEAD

A nylon lead is probably the best option, as it is the most resistant to puppy teeth should your pup take a liking to chewing on his lead. Of course, this is a habit that should be nipped in the bud, but, if your pup likes to chew on his lead, he has a very slim chance of being able to chew through the strong nylon. Nylon leads are also lightweight, which is good for a young Spinone who is just getting used to the idea of walking on a lead. For everyday walking and safety purposes, the nylon lead is a good choice. As your pup grows up and gets used to walking on the lead, you may want to purchase a flexible lead. These leads allow you to extend the length to give the dog a broader area to explore or to shorten the length to keep the dog near you. Of course, there are leads designed for training purposes and specially made leather harnesses, but these are not necessary for routine walks.

COLLAR

Your pup should get used to wearing a collar all the time since you will want to attach his ID tags to it; plus, you have to attach the lead to something! A lightweight nylon collar is a good choice. Make certain that the collar fits

Your local pet shop sells an array of dishes and bowls suitable for water and food.

PHOTO COURTESY OF MIKKI PET PRODUCTS.

snugly enough so that the pup cannot wriggle out of it, but is loose enough so that it will not be uncomfortably tight around the pup's neck. You should be able to fit a finger between the pup's neck and the collar. It may take some time for your pup to get used to wearing the collar, but soon he will not even notice that it is there. Choke collars are made for training, but should *only* be used by experienced handlers and is too harsh a method for the sensitive Spinone.

FOOD AND WATER BOWLS

Your pup will need two bowls, one for food and one for water. You may want two sets of bowls, one for indoors and one for outdoors, depending on where the dog will be fed and where he will be spending time. Stainless steel or sturdy plastic bowls are popular choices. Plastic bowls are more chewable, but dogs tend not to chew on the steel variety, which can be sterilised. It is important to buy sturdy bowls since anything is in danger of being chewed by puppy teeth and you do not want your dog to be constantly chewing apart his bowl (for his safety and for your purse!). Since the Spinone is prone to bloat, elevating his bowls with a bowl stand is an excellent way to avoid his craning his neck to eat, thus reducing the risk.

CHOOSE AN APPROPRIATE COLLAR

The **BUCKLE COLLAR** is the standard collar used for everyday purposes. Be sure that you adjust the buckle on growing puppies. Check it every day. It can become too tight overnight! These collars can be made of leather or nylon. Attach your dog's identification tags to this collar.

The **CHOKE COLLAR** is designed for training, but is not a good tool for the Spinone, who responds best to positive reinforcement. It is constructed of highly polished steel so that it slides easily through the stainless steel loop. The idea is that the dog controls the pressure around its neck and he will stop pulling if the collar becomes uncomfortable. It is worn *only* during training.

The **HALTER** is for a trained dog that has to be restrained to prevent running away, chasing a cat and the like. Considered the most humane of all collars, it is frequently used on smaller dogs for which collars are not comfortable.

It is your responsibility to clean up after your dog has relieved himself. Pet shops sell various aids to assist in the cleanup job.

Spinone puppies need to chew, so give the pup plenty of toys and keep your shoes in a safe place!

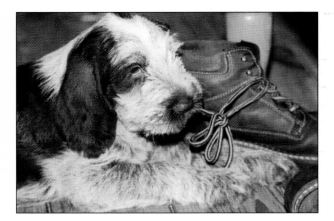

CLEANING SUPPLIES

Until a pup is house-trained, you will be doing a lot of cleaning. 'Accidents' will occur, which is acceptable in the beginning stages of toilet training because the puppy does not know any better. All you can do is be prepared to clean up any accidents as soon as they happen. Old rags, towels, newspapers and a safe disinfectant are good to have on hand.

BEYOND THE BASICS

The items previously discussed are the bare necessities. You will find out what else you need as you go along—grooming supplies, flea/tick protection, baby gates to partition a room, etc. These things will vary depending on your situation, but it is important that you have everything you need to feed and make your Spinone comfortable in his first few days at home.

PUPPY-PROOFING YOUR HOME

Aside from making sure that your Spinone will be comfortable in your home, you also have to make sure that your home is safe for your Spinone. This means taking precautions that your pup will not get into anything he should not get into and that there is nothing within his reach that may harm him should he sniff it, chew it, inspect it, etc. This probably seems obvious since, while you are primarily concerned with your pup's safety, at the same time you do not want your belongings to be ruined. Breakables should be placed out of reach if your dog is to have full run of the house. If he is to be limited to certain places within the house, keep any potentially dangerous items in the 'off-limits' areas.

An electrical cord can pose a danger should the puppy decide to taste it—and who is going to convince a pup that it would not make a great chew toy? Cords should be fastened tightly against the wall. If your dog is going to spend time in a crate, make sure that there is nothing near his crate that he can reach if he sticks his curious little nose or paws through the openings. Just as you would with a child, keep all household cleaners and chemicals where the pup cannot reach them.

It is also important to make sure that the outside of your home is safe. Of course, your puppy should never be unsupervised, but a pup let loose in the garden will want to run and explore, and he should be granted that freedom. Do not let a fence give you a false sense of security; you would be surprised at how crafty (and persistent) a dog can be in working out how to dig under and squeeze his way through small holes, or to jump or climb over a fence. With nothing else to do, the neglected Spinone can dig itself a hole that will make you think it is on a journey to the centre of the earth. The remedy is to make the fence well embedded into the ground and high enough so that it really is impossible for your dog

NATURAL TOXINS
Examine your grass and garden landscaping before bringing your puppy home. Many varieties of plants have leaves, stems or flowers that are toxic if ingested, and you can depend on a curious puppy to investigate them. Ask your vet for information on poisonous plants or research them at your library.

to get over it (about 2 metres should suffice). Be sure to repair or secure any gaps in the fence. Check the fence periodically to ensure that it is in good shape and make repairs as needed; a very determined pup may return to the same spot to 'work on it' until he is able to get through.

FIRST TRIP TO THE VET
You have selected your puppy, and your home and family are ready. Now all you have to do is collect your Spinone from the breeder and the fun begins, right?

A natural field dog, the Spinone will carefully explore every patch of greenery on your property.

Well…not so fast. Something else you need to plan is your pup's first trip to the veterinary surgeon. Perhaps the breeder can recommend someone in the area who specialises in field dogs, or maybe you know some other Spinone owners who can suggest a knowledgeable vet. Either way, you should have an appointment arranged for your pup before you pick him up.

The pup's first visit will consist of an overall examination to make sure that the pup does not have any problems that are not apparent to you. The veterinary surgeon will also set up a schedule for the pup's vaccinations; the breeder will inform you of which ones the pup has already received and the vet can continue from there.

INTRODUCTION TO THE FAMILY

Everyone in the house will be excited about the puppy's coming home and will want to pet him and play with him, but it is best to make the introductions low-key so as not to overwhelm the puppy. He is apprehensive already. It is the first time he has been separated from his mother and the breeder, and the ride to your home is likely to be the first time he has been in a car. The last thing you want to do is smother him, as this will only frighten him further. This is not to say that human contact is not extremely necessary at this stage, because this is the time when a connection between the pup and his human family is formed. Gentle petting and soothing words should help console him, as well as just putting him down and letting him explore on his own (under your watchful eye, of course).

The pup may approach the family members or may busy himself with exploring for a while. Gradually, each person should spend some time with the pup, one at a time, crouching down to get as close to the pup's level as possible, letting him sniff their hands and petting him gently. He definitely needs human attention and he needs to be touched—this is how to form an immediate bond. Just remember that the pup is experiencing many things for the first time, at the same time. There are new people, new noises, new smells and new things to investigate, so be gentle, be affectionate and be as comforting as you can be.

PUP'S FIRST NIGHT HOME

You have travelled home with your new charge safely in his crate or on a friend's lap. He's been to the vet for a thorough check-up; he's been weighed, his papers have been examined and perhaps he's even been vaccinated and wormed as well. He's met (and licked!) the whole family, including the excited children and the less-than-happy cat. He's explored his area, his new bed, the garden and anywhere else he's been permitted. He's eaten his first meal at home and relieved himself in the proper place. He's heard lots of new sounds, smelled new friends and seen more of the outside world than ever before... and that was just the first day! He's worn out and is ready for bed...or so you think!

It's puppy's first night home and you are ready to say 'Good night.' Keep in mind that this is his first night ever to be sleeping alone. His dam and littermates are

PUPPY-PROOFING
Thoroughly puppy-proof your house before bringing your puppy home. Never use cockroach or rodent poisons in any area accessible to the puppy. Avoid the use of toilet cleaners. Most dogs are born with 'toilet sonar' and will take a drink if the lid is left open. Also keep the rubbish secured and out of reach.

HOW VACCINES WORK

If you've just bought a puppy, you surely know the importance of having your pup vaccinated, but do you understand how vaccines work? Vaccines contain the same bacteria or viruses that cause the disease you want to prevent, but they have been chemically modified so that they don't cause any harm. Instead, the vaccine causes your dog to produce antibodies that fight the harmful bacteria. Thus, if your pup is exposed to the disease in the future, the antibodies will destroy the viruses or bacteria.

placing a piece of bedding from the pup's former home in his new bed so that he recognises and is comforted by the scent of his littermates. Others still advise placing a hot water bottle in the bed for warmth. The latter may be a good idea provided the pup doesn't attempt to suckle—he'll get good and wet, and may not fall asleep so fast.

Puppy's first night can be somewhat stressful for both the pup and his new family. Remember that you are setting the tone of night-time at your house. Unless you want to play with your pup every night at 10 p.m., midnight and 2 a.m., don't initiate the habit. Your family will thank you, and so will your pup!

PREVENTING PUPPY PROBLEMS

SOCIALISATION

Now that you have done all of the preparatory work and have helped your pup get accustomed to his new home and family, it is about time for you to have some fun! Socialising your Spinone pup gives you the opportunity to show off your new friend, and your pup gets to reap the benefits of being an adorable furry creature that people will want to pet and, in general, think is absolutely precious!

Besides getting to know his new family, your puppy should be

no longer at paw's length and he's a bit scared, cold and lonely. Be reassuring to your new family member, but this is not the time to spoil him and give in to his inevitable whining.

Puppies whine. They whine to let others know where they are and hopefully to get company out of it. Place your pup in his new bed or crate in his designated area and close the door. Mercifully, he may fall asleep without a peep. When the inevitable occurs, however, ignore the whining—he is fine. Be strong and keep his interests in mind. Do not allow yourself to feel guilty and visit the pup. He will fall asleep eventually.

Many breeders recommend

THE RIDE HOME

Taking your dog from the breeder to your home in a car can be a very uncomfortable experience for both of you. The puppy will have been taken from his warm, friendly, safe environment and brought into a strange new environment—an environment that moves! Be prepared for loose bowels, urination, crying, whining and even fear biting. With proper love and encouragement when you arrive home, the stress of the trip should quickly disappear.

socialisation, and/or negative experiences during the socialisation period, can manifest itself in fear and aggression as the dog grows up. Your puppy needs lots of positive interaction, which of course includes human contact, affection, handling and exposure to other animals.

Once your pup has received his necessary vaccinations, feel

STRESS-FREE

Some experts in canine health advise that stress during a dog's early years of development can compromise and weaken his immune system, and may trigger the potential for a shortened life expectancy. They emphasise the need for happy and stress-free growing-up years.

exposed to other people, animals and situations. This will help him become better adjusted as he grows up and less prone to being timid or fearful of the new things he will encounter. Of course, he must not come into close contact with dogs you don't know well until his course of injections is fully complete.

Your pup's socialisation began with the breeder, but now it is your responsibility to continue it. The socialisation he receives until the age of 12 weeks is the most critical, as this is the time when he forms his impressions of the outside world. Be especially careful during the eight-to-ten-week-old period, also known as the fear period. The interaction he receives during this time should be gentle and reassuring. Lack of

MANNERS MATTER

During the socialisation process, a puppy should meet people, experience different environments and definitely be exposed to other canines. Through playing and interacting with other dogs, your puppy will learn lessons, ranging from controlling the pressure of his jaws by biting his littermates to the inner-workings of the canine pack that he will apply to his human relationships for the rest of his life. That is why removing a puppy from its litter too early (before eight weeks) can be detrimental to the pup's development.

experiences positive ones. What a pup learns during this very formative stage will affect his attitude toward future encounters. You want your dog to be comfortable around everyone. A pup that has a bad experience with a child may grow up to be a dog that is shy around or aggressive toward children.

CONSISTENCY IN TRAINING

Dogs, being pack animals, naturally need a leader, or else they try to establish dominance in their packs. When you welcome a dog into your family, the choice of who becomes the leader and who becomes the 'pack' is entirely up to you! Your pup's intuitive quest for dominance, coupled with the fact that it is nearly impossible to look at an

free to take him out and about (on his lead, of course). Walk him around the neighbourhood, take him on your daily errands, let people pet him, let him meet other dogs and pets, etc. Puppies do not have to try to make friends; there will be no shortage of people who will want to introduce themselves. Just make sure that you carefully supervise each meeting. If the neighbourhood children want to say hello, for example, that is great—children and pups most often make great companions. However, sometimes an excited child can unintentionally handle a pup too roughly, or an overzealous pup can playfully nip a little too hard. You want to make socialisation

MEET THE WORLD

Thorough socialisation includes not only meeting new people but also being introduced to new experiences such as riding in the car, having his coat brushed, hearing the television, walking in a crowd—the list is endless. The more your pup experiences, and the more positive the experiences are, the less of a shock and the less frightening it will be for your pup to encounter new things.

A FORTNIGHT'S GRACE

It will take at least two weeks for your puppy to become accustomed to his new surroundings. Give him lots of love, attention, handling, frequent opportunities to relieve himself, a diet he likes to eat and a place he can call his own.

old saying 'You can't teach an old dog new tricks' does not necessarily hold true, but it is true that it is much easier to discourage bad behaviour in a young developing pup than to wait until the pup's bad behaviour becomes the adult dog's bad habit. There are some problems that are especially prevalent in puppies as they develop.

adorable Spinone pup with his 'puppy-dog' eyes and not cave in, give the pup almost an unfair advantage in getting the upper hand! A pup will definitely test the waters to see what he can and cannot do. Do not give in to those pleading eyes—stand your ground when it comes to disciplining the pup and make sure that all family members do the same. It will only confuse the pup if Mother tells him to get off the sofa when he is used to sitting up there with Father to watch the nightly news. Avoid discrepancies by having all members of the household decide on the rules before the pup even comes home...and be consistent in enforcing them! Early training shapes the dog's personality, so you cannot be unclear in what you expect.

PROPER SOCIALISATION

The socialisation period for puppies is from age 8 to 16 weeks. This is the time when puppies need to leave their birth family and take up residence with their new owners, where they will meet many new people, other pets, etc. Failure to be adequately socialised can cause the dog to grow up fearing others and being shy and unfriendly due to a lack of self-confidence.

COMMON PUPPY PROBLEMS

The best way to prevent puppy problems is to be proactive in stopping an undesirable behaviour as soon as it starts. The

Your pup's special area, with soft bedding so that he can cuddle up, will help him settle into his new home.

NIPPING

As puppies start to teethe, they feel the need to sink their teeth into anything available… unfortunately, that usually includes your fingers, arms, hair and toes. You may find this behaviour cute for the first five seconds…until you feel just how sharp those puppy teeth are. Nipping is something you want to discourage immediately and consistently with a firm 'No!' (or whatever number of firm 'Nos' it takes for him to understand that you mean business). Then, replace your finger with an appropriate chew toy. While this behaviour is merely annoying when the dog is young, it can become dangerous as your Spinone's adult teeth grow in and his jaws develop, and he continues to think it is okay to gnaw on human appendages. Your Spinone does not mean any harm with a friendly nip, but he also does not know his own strength.

CRYING/WHINING

Your pup will often cry, whine, whimper, howl or make some type of commotion when he is left alone. This is basically his way of calling out for attention to make sure that you know he is there and that you have not forgotten about him. Your puppy feels insecure when he is left alone, when you are out of the house and he is in his crate or when you are in another part of the house and he cannot see you. The noise he is making is an expression of the anxiety he feels at being alone, so he needs to be taught that being alone is okay. You are not actually training the dog to stop making noise; rather, you are training him to feel comfortable when he is alone and thus removing the need for him to make the noise. This is where the crate with cosy bedding and a toy comes in handy. You want to know that your pup is safe when

PUPPY PROBLEMS

The majority of problems that are commonly seen in young pups will disappear as your dog gets older. However, how you deal with problems when he is young will determine how he reacts to discipline as an adult dog. It is important to establish who is boss (hopefully it will be you!) right away when you are first bonding with your dog. This bond will set the tone for the rest of your life together.

you are not there to supervise, and you know that he will be safe in his crate rather than roaming freely about the house. In order for the pup to stay in his crate without making a fuss, he first needs to be comfortable in his crate. On that note, it is extremely important that the crate is never used as a form of punishment; this will cause the pup to view the crate as a negative place, rather than as a place of his own for safety and retreat.

Accustom the pup to the crate in short, gradually increasing time intervals in which you put him in the crate, maybe with a treat, and stay in the room with him. If he cries or makes a fuss, do not go to him, but stay in his sight. Gradually he will realise that staying in his crate is all right

without your help, and it will not be so traumatic for him when you are not around. You may want to leave the radio on softly when you leave the house; the sound of human voices may be comforting to him.

FEEDING YOUR SPINONE

If you ask a Spinone breeder or owner what and when you should feed your new puppy, he will surely tell you that a specific feeding schedule is critical and that a good rule of thumb is to feed the amount that the puppy, or adult for that matter, will eat in five minutes. (If you were to ask a Spinone that same question, the answer would undoubtedly be 'everything and always!') The recommended content may vary from breeder to breeder, but the five-minute rule is apt to remain constant.

Unlike the advice given to the new owners of many other breeds, the Spinone's food intake must be regulated carefully because Spinoni are hungry around the clock, and in most cases hungry for anything that even remotely resembles food! An overweight puppy or dog can quickly become the result. This puts stress on the kidneys and heart, to say nothing of the strain on a puppy's suscep-tible skeletal development.

After weaning and up to about three months of age, the Spinone puppy should be getting four meals a day. At that point, three meals a day are sufficient and, by the time the puppy is six months old, he might well be put on a morning/evening schedule. Here again, these are simply rules of thumb. The lean and leggy puppy might need a supplement to the morning/evening schedule. The too-pudgy puppy should be kept on the two-meal schedule, but perhaps fed a bit less at each.

Most breeders recommend keeping the Spinone on puppy food until about six to seven months of age. Depending upon individual dog and general condition (weight, activity, etc.), an active Spinone should be able to stay on a maintenance diet until he reaches that 'slow-down' point in his life; he then can be switched to a senior diet. Again, this varies from dog to dog.

Most commercial foods

TEST FOR PROPER DIET

A good test for proper diet is the colour, odour and firmness of your dog's stool. A healthy dog usually produces three semi-hard stools per day. The stools should have no unpleasant odour. They should be the same colour from excretion to excretion.

manufactured for dogs meet nutrition standards and list the ingredients contained in the food on every package and can. The ingredients are listed in descending order, with the main ingredient listed first. Refined sugars are not a part of the canine natural food acquisition, and

FEEDING TIP

You must store your dried dog food carefully. Open packages of dog food quickly lose their vitamin value, usually within 90 days of being opened. Mould spores and vermin could also contaminate the food.

canine teeth are not genetically disposed to handling these sugars. Do not feed your Spinone sugar products, and avoid products that contain sugar to any high degree.

Fresh water and a properly prepared, balanced diet containing the essential nutrients in correct proportions are all that a healthy Spinone needs to be offered. Dog foods come canned, dried, semi-moist, 'scientifically fortified' and 'all-natural.' A visit to your local pet store will reveal how vast an array you will be able to select from.

All dogs, whether large or small, are carnivorous (meat-eating) animals. Animal protein

FOOD PREFERENCE

Selecting the best dried dog food is difficult. There is no majority consensus among veterinary scientists as to the value of nutrient analyses (protein, fat, fibre, moisture, ash, cholesterol, minerals, etc.). All agree that feeding trials are what matter, but you also have to consider the individual dog. The dog's weight, age and activity level, and what pleases his taste, all must be considered. It is probably best to take the advice of your veterinary surgeon. Every dog's dietary requirements vary, even during the lifetime of a particular dog.

Dogs do appreciate a little variety in their diets, so you may choose to stay with the same brand of dried food but vary the flavour. Alternatively, you may wish to add a little flavoured stock to give a difference to the taste.

From birth to first taste of mother's milk...the photo shows the puppy being born in a placenta-filled sac.

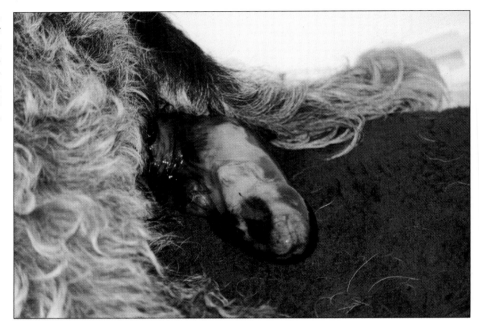

The mother bites through the umbilical cord to release the pup from the sac.

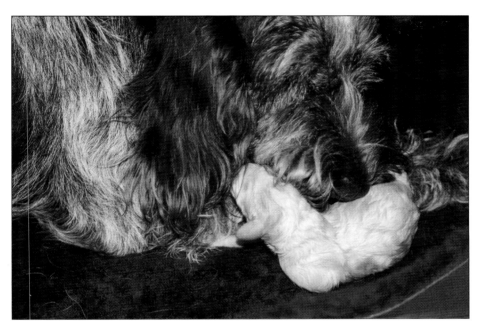

After eating the placenta, the dam licks the puppy dry.

Three minutes after birth, the puppy's eyes are not yet opened.

The pups seek out the mother's nipples and begin to suckle.

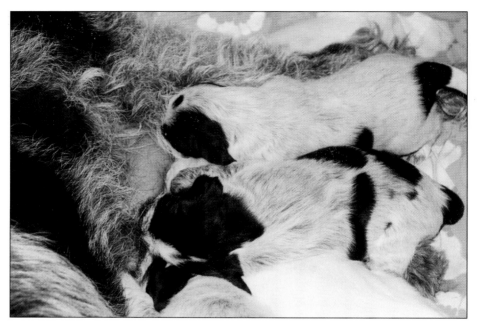

Mom and her newborn litter of hungry pups.

GRAIN-BASED DIETS

Some less expensive dog foods are based on grains and other plant proteins. While these products may appear to be attractively priced, many breeders prefer a diet based on animal proteins and believe that they are more conducive to your dog's health. Many grain-based diets rely on soy protein, which may cause flatulence (passing gas).

There are many cases, however, when your dog might require a special diet. These special requirements should only be recommended by your veterinary surgeon.

As the pups mature, the breeder introduces solid food as part of the weaning process.

and fats are essential to the well-being of your Spinone. However, a diet too high in proteins can lead to problems as well. Not all dried foods contain the necessary amount of protein that a Spinone requires to keep it in top condition. It is best to discuss this with the breeder from whom you purchase your dog or with your veterinary surgeon.

The domesticated dog's diet must include protein, carbohydrates, fats, roughage and small amounts of essential minerals and vitamins. Many breeders strongly recommend adding small amounts of cooked vegetables to a Spinone's diet. This provides the necessary carbohydrates, minerals and nutrients present only in vegetables.

Commercially prepared foods contain all of the necessary vitamins your Spinone needs. It is unnecessary, in fact inadvisable, to add vitamin supplements to these diets in other than special circumstances prescribed by your vet. Over-supplementation and forced growth are now looked upon by some breeders as major contributors to many skeletal abnormalities found in pure-bred dogs of the day. Some people may claim these problems and a wide

CHANGE IN DIET

As your dog's caretaker, you know the importance of keeping his diet consistent, but sometimes when you run out of food or if you're on holiday, you have to make a change quickly. Some dogs will experience digestive problems, but most will not. If you are planning on changing your dog's menu, do so gradually to ensure that your dog will not have any problems. Over a period of four to five days, slowly add some new food to your dog's old food, increasing the percentage of new food each day.

'DOES THIS COLLAR MAKE ME LOOK FAT?'

While humans may obsess about how they look and how trim their bodies are, many people believe that extra weight on their dogs is a good thing. The truth is, pets should not be over- or under-weight, as both can lead to or signal sickness. In order to tell how fit your pet is, run your hands over his ribs. Are his ribs buried under a layer of fat or are they sticking out considerably? If your pet is within his normal weight range, you should be able to feel the ribs easily, but they should not protrude abnormally. If you stand above him, the outline of his body should resemble an hourglass. Some breeds do tend to be leaner while some are a bit stockier, but making sure your dog is the right weight for his breed will certainly contribute to his good health.

variety of chronic skin conditions are entirely hereditary but many others feel they can be exacerbated by diet and over-use of mineral and vitamin supplements for puppies.

EXERCISE

Exercise is a bottom-line fact in a Spinone's life. The Spinone was bred to work day in and day out in the field, and that ability and need remain with the breed to this day. A well-exercised Spinone can live happily with just a reasonably-sized run in a big city, but understand the operative words

THE CANINE GOURMET

Your dog does not prefer a fresh bone. Indeed, he wants it properly aged and, if given such a treat indoors, he is more likely to try to bury it in the carpet than he is to settle in for a good chew! If you have a garden, give him such delicacies outside and guide him to a place suitable for his 'bone yard.' He will carefully place the treasure in its earthy vault and seemingly forget about it. Trust me, his seeming distaste or lack of thanks for your thoughtfulness is not that at all. He will return in a few days to inspect the bone, perhaps to re-bury it, and when it is just right, he will relish it as much as you do that cooked-to-perfection steak. If he is in a concrete or bricked kennel run, he will be especially frustrated at the hopelessness of the situation. He will vacillate between ignoring it completely, giving it a few licks to speed the curing process with saliva and trying to hide it behind the water bowl! When the bone has aged a bit, he will set to work on it.

Food is number-one on the Spinone's list of priorities, and if there's food to be found, he will find it and help himself! Keep 'people food' out of the dog's reach—food stealing is neither good behaviour nor good for the dog.

here are 'well-exercised.' That means full-out running on the beach or in the country several times a week at the very minimum. Do not expect that a short gallop in the park will suffice. If it is to be the park where your Spinone will get his exercise, consider who will keep

What are you feeding your dog?

Read the label on your dog food. Many dog foods only advise what 50—55% of the contents are, leaving the other 45% in doubt.

Calcium 1.3%
Fatty Acids 1.6%
Crude Fibre 4.6%
Moisture 11%
Crude Fat 14%
Crude Protein 22%
45.5% ? ? ?

an eye out for toddlers or 'little fluffies' who are going about their own business. Particularly when the Spinone is running free, those little objects entice him to give chase.

Mature Spinoni are capable and delighted to be jogging companions. It is important, however, to use good judgement in any exercise programme. Begin slowly and increase the distance to be covered very gradually over

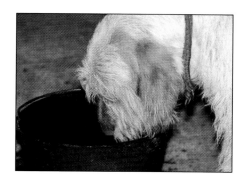

Water is as necessary to the dog's well-being as his diet...and a thirsty Spinone will drink it by the bucketful!

an extended period of time. Use special precautions in hot weather. High temperatures and forced exercise are a dangerous combination.

Since the growing frames of young dogs are susceptible to injury, puppies should never be forced to exercise. Normally, they are little dynamos of energy and keep themselves busy all day long, interspersed with frequent naps. Never expose puppies to strenuous activities or exercise.

The best exercise for a Spinone is that which he acquires in the pursuit of the very thing the breed was created for—field work. There is no better way to ensure your Spinone of a happy, healthy existence.

GROOMING YOUR SPINONE

BRUSHING AND COAT MAINTENANCE
The Spinone is a natural breed that requires only minor clipping and neatening around the tail, legs and feet. Thinning shears are

Your local pet shop will have a variety of grooming tools from which you can select what you need to maintain your Spinone's coat.

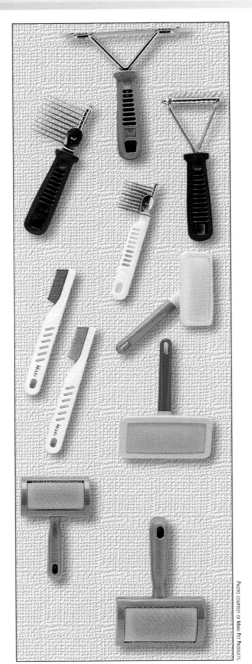

excellent for this purpose. Invest in a quality pair of thinning shears, a slicker or pinbrush and a good natural bristle brush that has some nylon bristles inserted in it. You will also need a steel comb to remove any debris that collects in the longer furnishings. A comb that has teeth divided between fine and coarse is ideal. All of these supplies are available at the local pet shop.

Regular thorough brushing with the slicker or pinbrush to keep the coat and furnishings tangle-free should be part of a regular routine. Follow this with a stimulating brush-down with the bristle brush. Together, those operations will keep both the coat and skin clean and healthy. If a

GROOMING EQUIPMENT

How much grooming equipment you purchase will depend on how much grooming you are going to do. Here are some basics:

- Bristle brush
- Slicker or pinbrush
- Thinning shears
- Metal comb
- Stripping knife
- Blaster
- Rubber mat
- Dog shampoo
- Spray hose attachment
- Ear cleaner
- Cotton wipes
- Towels
- Nail clippers

Use of a grooming table raises the dog to a comfortable height for the groomer to work, while keeping the dog secure and still during the process.

Every part of the Spinone should be groomed, even the sensitive areas, which require careful and gentle attention.

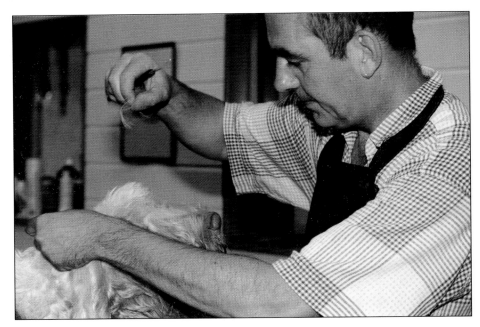

Hand-stripping is an art that takes time and practice to learn and perfect.

mat or tangle should develop and you find you can't work it apart with your fingers and a steel comb, use the thinning shears to help separate the mat.

The longer hair of the ears and beard will attract food and debris. Use a metal comb especially for dogs for this purpose. Frequent bathing is suggested for these two areas. This will keep debris from collecting and avoid foul smells from developing. You can dry bath your Spinone by sprinkling a little baby powder in the coat and then working it well in and brushing it out. This, of course, also helps to make the dog smell very good. Over-bathing can lead

to dry-skin problems. Dry skin creates a need to scratch and this can lead to severe scratching and 'hot spots,' moist sore areas in which the coat is entirely scratched away.

The easiest way to groom a Spinone is by placing the dog on a grooming table or elevated platform. Make sure the dog is at a height at which you can work comfortably either sitting or standing. Adjustable-height grooming tables are available at most pet outlets and are well worth the initial investment. It is best to use a grooming table that has an 'arm' and a 'noose.' The noose slips around the dog's neck when it is standing and keeps the dog from fidgeting about or jumping down when he has decided he has had enough grooming. However, do not leave your dog alone when you are using the noose, even for a few minutes. Your dog could jump or fall off the table and injure himself.

When brushing, proceed vigorously from behind the head to the tail. Do this all over the body and be especially careful to attend to the hard-to-reach areas between the legs, behind the ears and under the body. Mats can occur, particularly when the dog is moulting or when the coat catches burrs or sticky substances in its longer furnishings. Should you encounter a mat that does not brush out easily, use your fingers and the steel comb to separate the hairs as much as possible. Do not cut or pull out the matted hair. Apply baby powder or one of the especially prepared grooming powders directly to the mat and brush completely from the skin out.

The coat of a neutered Spinone, male or female, will be softer and longer than that of entire dogs. It is helpful to strip the coat of a neutered Spinone two or three time a year to keep the coat harsher and in a more natural prickly state. A stripping knife is used for this purpose and the breeder from which the Spinone is purchased can instruct most any owner how to accomplish the procedure.

DRINK, DRANK, DRUNK— MAKE IT A DOUBLE

In both humans and dogs, as well as most living organisms, water forms the major part of nearly every body tissue. Naturally, we take water for granted, but without it, life as we know it would cease.

For dogs, water is needed to keep their bodies functioning biochemically. Additionally, water is needed to replace the water lost while panting. Unlike humans, who are able to sweat to dissipate heat, dogs must pant to cool down, thereby losing the vital water from their bodies needed to regulate their body temperatures. Humans lose electrolyte-containing products and other body-fluid components through sweating; dogs do not lose anything except water.

Water is essential always, but especially so when the weather is hot or humid or when your dog is exercising or working vigorously.

SOAP IT UP

The use of human soap products like shampoo, bubble bath and hand soap can be damaging to a dog's coat and skin. Human products are too strong; they remove the protective oils coating the dog's hair and skin that make him water-resistant. Use only shampoo made especially for dogs. You may like to use a medicated shampoo, which will help to keep external parasites at bay.

BATHING

Dogs do not need to be bathed as often as humans, but regular bathing is essential for healthy skin and a healthy, shiny coat. Again, like most anything, if you accustom your pup to being bathed as a puppy, it will be second nature by the time he grows up. You want your dog to be at ease in the bath or else it could end up a wet, soapy, messy ordeal for both of you!

Brush your Spinone thoroughly before wetting his coat. This will get rid of most mats and tangles, which are harder to remove when the coat is wet. Make certain that your dog has a good non-slip surface on which to stand. Begin by wetting the dog's coat, checking the water temperature to make sure that it is neither too hot nor too cold. A shower or hose attachment is necessary for thoroughly wetting and rinsing the coat.

Next, apply shampoo to the dog's coat and work it into a good lather. Wash the head last, as you do not want shampoo to drip into the dog's eyes while you are washing the rest of his body. You should use only a shampoo that is made for dogs. Do not use a product made for human hair. Work the shampoo all the way down to the skin. You can use this opportunity to check the skin for any bumps, bites or other abnormalities. Do not neglect any area of the body—get all of the hard-to-reach places.

Once the dog has been thoroughly shampooed, he

BATHING BEAUTY

Once you are sure that the dog is thoroughly rinsed, squeeze the excess water out of his coat with your hand and dry him with a heavy towel. You may choose to use a blaster on his coat or just let it dry naturally. In cold weather, never allow your dog outside with a wet coat.

There are 'dry bath' products on the market, which are sprays and powders intended for spot cleaning, that can be used between regular baths if necessary. They are not substitutes for regular baths, but they are easy to use for touch-ups as they do not require rinsing.

requires an equally thorough rinsing. Shampoo left in the coat can be irritating to the dog's skin. Protect his eyes from the shampoo by shielding them with your hand and directing the flow of water in the opposite direction. You should also avoid getting water in the ear canal. Be prepared for your dog to shake out his coat— you might want to stand back, but make sure you have a hold on the dog to keep him from running through the house.

NAIL TRIMMING

The grooming session is a good time to accustom your Spinone to having his nails trimmed and feet inspected. Always inspect your dog's feet for cracked pads. Check between the toes for splinters and thorns that may be embedded in the soft hair between the pads and toes. Pay particular attention to any swollen or tender areas.

We suggest attending to your dog's nails at least every three to four weeks. Long nails spread and weaken the foot. The nails of a Spinone that isn't exercising on rough terrain will grow long very quickly.

Each nail has a blood vessel running through the centre called the 'quick.' The quick grows close to the end of the nail and contains very sensitive nerve endings. If the nail is allowed to grow too long it will be impossible to cut it back to a proper length without

THAT'S ENTERTAINMENT!

Is your dog home alone for much of the day? If you haven't taught him how to crochet or play the French horn, then he'll need something to occupy his paws and jaws, lest he turn to chewing up the carpet and draperies. Recommended conditioning devices are toys that stimulate your dog both physically and mentally. Some of the most popular toys are those that are constructed to hide food inside. They provide not only a challenge but also instant gratification when your dog gets to the treat. Be sure to clean these carefully to prevent bacteria from building up.

cutting into the quick. This causes severe pain to the dog and can also result in a great deal of bleeding that can be difficult to stop.

Nails can be trimmed with canine nail clippers or an electric

Clip your
Spinone's nails
every three to
four weeks.

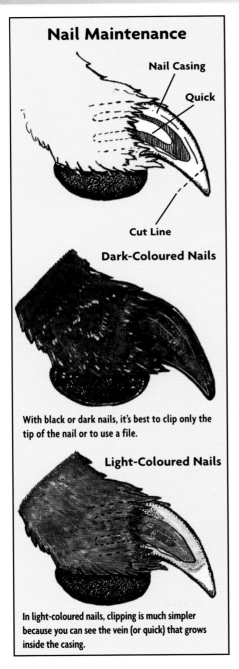

Nail Maintenance

Nail Casing

Quick

Cut Line

Dark-Coloured Nails

With black or dark nails, it's best to clip only the tip of the nail or to use a file.

Light-Coloured Nails

In light-coloured nails, clipping is much simpler because you can see the vein (or quick) that grows inside the casing.

nail grinder called a drummel. Use the 'fine' grinding disc on the drummel because this allows you to trim back the nail a little bit at a time, practically eliminating the chance of any bleeding. Always proceed with caution and remove only a small portion of the nail at a time. Should the quick be nipped in the trimming process, there are any number of blood-clotting products available at pet shops that will almost immediately stem the flow of blood. It is

NAIL FILING

You can purchase an electric tool to grind down a dog's nails rather than cut them. Some dogs don't seem to mind the electric grinder but will object strongly to nail clippers. Talking it over with your veterinary surgeon will help you make the right choice.

wise to have one of these products on hand in case your dog breaks a nail in some way.

EAR CLEANING

The ears should be kept clean with a cotton wipe and ear powder made especially for dogs. Do not probe into the ear canal with a cotton bud, as this can cause injury. Be on the lookout for any signs of infection or ear-mite infestation. If your Spinone has been shaking his head or scratching at his ears frequently, this usually indicates a problem. If the dog's ears have an unusual odour, this is a sure sign of mite infestation or infection, and a signal to have his ears checked by the veterinary surgeon.

TRAVELLING WITH YOUR DOG

CAR TRAVEL

You should accustom your Spinone to riding in a car at an early age. You may or may not take him in the car often, but at the very least he will need to go to the vet and you do not want these trips to be traumatic for the dog or troublesome for you. The safest way for a dog to ride in the car is in his crate. If he uses a crate in the house, you can use the same crate for travel.

Put the pup in the crate and see how he reacts. If he seems uneasy, you can have a passenger hold him on his lap while you

ON THE ROAD
If you are going on a long motor trip with your dog, be sure the hotels are dog-friendly. Many hotels do not accept dogs. Also take along some ice that can be thawed and offered to your dog if he becomes overheated. Most dogs like to lick ice.

drive. Another option for car travel is a specially made safety harness for dogs, which straps the dog in much like a seat belt. Do not let the dog roam loose in the vehicle—this is very dangerous! If you should stop short, your dog can be thrown and injured. If the dog starts climbing on you and pestering you while you are driving, you will not be able to concentrate on the road. It is an unsafe situation for everyone— human and canine.

For long trips, be prepared to stop to let the dog relieve himself. Take with you whatever you need to clean up after him, including some paper kitchen towels and perhaps some old towelling for use should he have a toileting accident in the car or suffer from travel sickness.

AIR TRAVEL

While it is possible to take a dog on a flight within Britain, this is fairly unusual and advance

MOTION SICKNESS

*If life is a motorway...*your dog may not want to come along for the ride! Some dogs experience motion sickness in cars that leads to excessive salivation and even vomiting. In most cases, your dog will fare better in the familiar, safe confines of his crate. To desensitise your dog, try going on several short jaunts before trying a long trip. If your dog experiences distress when riding in the vehicle, drive with him only when absolutely necessary, and do not feed him or give him water before you go.

permission is always required. The dog will be required to travel in a fibreglass crate and you

should always check in advance with the airline regarding specific requirements. To help put the dog at ease, give him one of his favourite toys in the crate. Do not feed the dog for at least six hours before the trip in order to minimise his need to relieve himself. However, certain regulations specify that water must always be made available to the

TRAVEL TIP

When travelling, never let your dog off-lead in a strange area. Your dog could run away out of fear, decide to chase a passing squirrel or cat or simply want to stretch his legs without restriction—if any of these happen, you might never see your canine friend again.

dog in the crate.

Make sure your dog is properly identified and that your contact information appears on his ID tags and on his crate. Animals travel in a different area of the plane than human passengers, so every rule must be strictly followed so as to prevent the risk of getting separated from your dog.

Never drive with your Spinone unrestrained in the car. Crates, harnesses and partitions for the back of the vehicle are several safety options available for your dog.

BOARDING

So you want to take a family holiday—and you want to include *all* members of the family. You would probably make arrangements for accommodation ahead of time anyway, but this is especially important when travelling with a dog. You do not want to make an overnight stop at the only place around for miles, only to find out that they do not allow dogs. Also, you do not want to reserve a place for your family without confirming that you are travelling with a dog, because, if it is against their policy, you may end up without a place to stay.

Alternatively, if you are travelling and choose not to bring your Spinone, you will have to make arrangements for him while you are away. Some options are to take him to a neighbour's house to stay while you are gone, to have a trusted neighbour pop in often or stay at your house or to bring your dog to a reputable boarding kennel. If you choose to board him at a kennel, you should visit in advance to see the facilities provided and where the dogs are kept. Are the dogs' areas spacious and kept clean? Talk to some of the employees and observe how they treat the dogs—do they spend time with the dogs, play with them, exercise them, etc.? Also find out the kennel's policy on vaccinations and what they require. This is for all of the dogs' safety, since there is a greater risk of diseases being passed from dog to dog when dogs are kept together.

ABUSING YOUR BEST FRIEND

As an educated and caring pet owner, you may believe that everyone wants to invest countless hours (and pounds) in order to raise a loving and well-adjusted canine companion. Sadly, this is not the case, as dogs account for almost half of all victims of animal abuse. Remember, abuse implies not only beating or torturing an animal but also neglecting the animal, such as failing to provide adequate shelter and food or emotional fulfilment.

IDENTIFICATION

Your Spinone is your valued companion and friend. That is why you always keep a close eye on him and you have made sure that he cannot escape from the garden or wriggle out of his collar and run away from you. However, accidents can happen and there may come a time when your dog unexpectedly becomes separated from you. If this unfortunate event should occur, the first thing on your mind will be finding him. Proper identification, including an ID tag, a tattoo and possibly a microchip, will increase the chances of his being returned to you safely and quickly.

Identification
tattoo inside the
Spinone's ear
flap.

Microchip
implantation can
be performed by
your vet. Many
breeders consider
it the most
reliable method
to identify a dog.

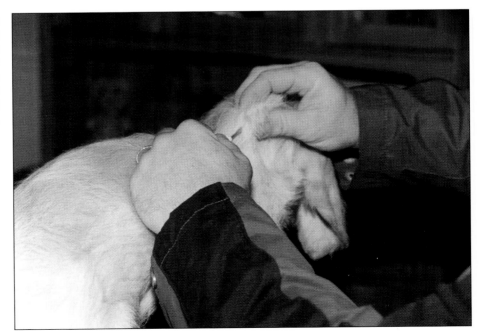

Be certain that your dog's ID tag is securely fastened to his everyday collar.

COLLAR REQUIRED

If your dog gets lost, he is not able to ask for directions home. Identification tags fastened to the collar give important information—the dog's name, the owner's name, the owner's address and a telephone number where the owner can be reached. This makes it easy for whomever finds the dog to contact the owner and arrange to have the dog returned. An added advantage is that a person will be more likely to approach a lost dog who has ID tags on his collar; it tells the person that this is somebody's pet rather than a stray. This is the easiest and fastest method of identification, provided that the tags stay on the collar and the collar stays on the dog.

IDENTIFICATION OPTIONS

As puppies become more and more expensive, especially those puppies of high quality for showing and/or breeding, they have a greater chance of being stolen. The usual collar dog tag is, of course, easily removed. But there are two more permanent techniques that have become widely used for identification.

The puppy microchip implantation involves the injection of a small microchip, about the size of a corn kernel, under the skin of the dog. If your dog shows up at a clinic or shelter, or is offered for resale under less than savoury circumstances, it can be positively identified by the microchip. The microchip is scanned, and a registry quickly identifies you as the owner. This is not only protection against theft, but should the dog run away or go chasing a squirrel and become lost, you have a fair chance of his being returned to you.

Tattooing is done on various parts of the dog, from his belly to his cheeks. The number tattooed can be your telephone number or any other number that you can easily memorise. When professional dog thieves see a tattooed dog, they usually lose interest. Both microchipping and tattooing can be done at your local veterinary clinic. For the safety of our dogs, no laboratory facility or dog broker will accept a tattooed dog as stock.

Living with an untrained dog is a lot like owning a piano that you do not know how to play—it is a nice object to look at but it does not do much more than that to bring you pleasure. Now try taking piano lessons, and suddenly the piano comes alive and brings forth magical sounds and rhythms that set your heart singing and your body swaying.

The same is true with your Spinone. Any dog is a big responsibility and, if not trained sensibly, may develop unacceptable behaviour that annoys you or could even cause family friction. Remember that the Spinone is an immensely gifted dog, with intelligence superior to most other breeds. It will take a dedicated and clever trainer to convince the Spinone that every lesson is valuable. Spinoni despise repetition, so be concise and focused when beginning your Spinone's education.

To train your Spinone, you may like to enrol in an obedience class. Teach your dog good manners as you learn how and why he behaves the way he does.

Find out how to communicate with your dog and how to recognise and understand his communications with you. Suddenly the dog takes on a new

role in your life—he is clever, interesting, well behaved and fun to be with. He demonstrates his bond of devotion to you daily. In other words, your Spinone does wonders for your ego because he constantly reminds you that you are not only his leader, you are his hero!

Those involved with teaching dog obedience and counselling owners about their dogs' behaviour have discovered some interesting facts about dog

PARENTAL GUIDANCE
Training a dog is a life experience. Many parents admit that much of what they know about raising children they learned from caring for their dogs. Dogs respond to love, fairness and guidance, just as children do. Become a good dog owner and you may become an even better parent.

ownership. For example, training dogs when they are puppies results in the highest rate of success in developing well-mannered and well-adjusted adult dogs. Training an older dog, from six months to six years of age, can produce almost equal results providing that the owner accepts the dog's slower rate of learning capability and is willing to work patiently to help the dog succeed at developing to his fullest potential. Unfortunately, many owners of untrained adult dogs lack the patience factor, so they do not persist until their dogs are successful at learning particular behaviours.

Training a puppy aged 10 to 16 weeks (20 weeks at the most) is like working with a dry sponge in a pool of water. The pup soaks up

The Spinone is an intelligent and loyal breed that responds to its master and to positive methods of training.

REAP THE REWARDS

If you start with a normal, healthy dog and give him time, patience and some carefully executed lessons, you will reap the rewards of that training for the life of the dog. And what a life it will be! The two of you will find immeasurable pleasure in the companionship you have built together with love, respect and understanding.

whatever you show him and constantly looks for more things to do and learn. At this early age, his body is not yet producing hormones, and therein lies the reason for such a high rate of success. Without hormones, he is focused on his owners and not particularly interested in investigating other places, dogs, people, etc. You are his leader: his provider of food, water, shelter and security. He latches onto you and wants to stay close. He will usually follow you from room to room, will not let you out of his sight when you are outdoors with him and will respond in like manner to the people and animals you encounter. If you greet a friend warmly, he will be happy to greet the person as well. If, however, you are hesitant or anxious about the approach of a stranger, he will respond accordingly.

Once the puppy begins to produce hormones, his natural curiosity emerges and he begins to investigate the world around him. It is at this time when you may notice that the untrained dog begins to wander away from you and even ignore your commands to stay close. When this behaviour becomes a problem, you have two choices: get rid of the dog or train him. It is strongly urged that you choose the latter option.

You usually will be able to find obedience classes within a

reasonable distance from your home, but you can also do a lot to train your dog yourself. Sometimes there are classes available, but the tuition is too costly. Whatever the circumstances, the solution to training your dog without obedience classes lies within the pages of this book.

This chapter is devoted to helping you train your Spinone at home. If the recommended procedures are followed faithfully, you may expect positive results that will prove rewarding both to you and your dog.

Whether your new charge is a puppy or a mature adult, the methods of teaching and the techniques we use in training basic behaviours are the same. After all, no dog, whether puppy or adult, likes harsh or inhumane methods, especially a sensitive breed like the Spinone. All creatures, however, respond favourably to gentle motivational

THINK BEFORE YOU BARK
Dogs are sensitive to their masters' moods and emotions. Use your voice wisely when communicating with your dog. Never raise your voice at your dog unless you are angry and trying to correct him. 'Barking' at your dog can become as meaningless as 'dogspeak' is to you. Think before you bark!

HONOUR AND OBEY
Dogs are the most honourable animals in existence. They consider another species (humans) as their own. They interface with you. You are their leader. Puppies perceive children to be on their level; their actions around small children are different from their behaviour around their adult masters.

methods and sincere praise and encouragement. Now let us get started.

TOILET TRAINING
You can train a puppy to relieve himself wherever you choose, but this must be somewhere suitable. You should bear in mind from the outset that when your puppy is old enough to go out in public places, any canine deposits must be removed at once. You will

always have to carry with you a small plastic bag or 'poop-scoop.'

Outdoor training includes such surfaces as grass, gravel, and cement. Indoor training usually means training your dog to newspaper. When deciding on the surface and location that you will want your Spinone to use, be sure it is going to be permanent. Training your dog to grass and then changing your mind a few months later is extremely difficult for both dog and owner.

Puppies have no trouble finding trouble! Defining your pup's living space promotes good behaviour in that it lessens the risk of his getting into something he shouldn't.

Next, choose the command you will use each and every time you want your puppy to void. 'Hurry up' and 'Toilet' are examples of commands commonly used by dog owners. Get in the habit of giving the puppy your chosen relief command before you take him out. That way, when he becomes an adult, you will be able to determine if he wants to go out when you ask him. A confirmation will be signs of interest, wagging his tail, watching you intently, going to the door, etc.

MEALTIME
Mealtime should be a peaceful time for your puppy. Do not put his food and water bowls in a high-traffic area in the house. For example, give him his own little corner of the kitchen where he can eat undisturbed and where he will not be underfoot. Do not allow small children or other family members to disturb the pup when he is eating.

PUPPY'S NEEDS
Puppy needs to relieve himself after play periods, after each meal, after he has been sleeping and at any time he indicates that he is looking for a place to urinate or defecate. The urinary and intestinal tract muscles of very young puppies are not fully developed. Therefore, like human babies, puppies need to relieve themselves frequently.

Take your puppy out often—every hour for an eight-week-old, for example—and always immediately after sleeping and eating.

ATTENTION!
Your dog is actually training you at the same time you are training him. Dogs do things to get attention. They usually repeat whatever succeeds in getting your attention.

The older the puppy, the less often he will need to relieve himself. Finally, as a mature healthy adult, he will require only three to five relief trips per day.

HOUSING

Since the types of housing and control you provide for your puppy have a direct relationship on the success of house-training, we consider the various aspects of both before we begin training.

Taking a new puppy home and turning him loose in your house can be compared to turning a child loose in a sports arena and telling the child that the place is all his! The sheer enormity of the place would be too much for him to handle. Instead, offer the puppy clearly defined areas where he can play, sleep, eat and live. A room of the house where the family gathers is the most obvious choice. Puppies are social animals and need to feel a part of the pack right from the start. Hearing your voice, watching you while you are doing things and smelling you nearby are all positive reinforcers that he is now a member of your pack. Usually a family room, the kitchen or a nearby adjoining breakfast area is ideal for providing safety and security for both puppy and owner.

Within the designated room, there should be a smaller area that the puppy can call his own. An alcove, a wire or fibreglass dog crate or a fenced (not boarded!) corner from which he can view the activities of his new family will be fine. The size of the area

TRAINING TIP

Dogs will do anything for your attention. If you reward the dog when he is calm and resting, you will develop a well-mannered dog. If, on the other hand, you greet your dog excitedly and encourage him to wrestle with you, the dog will greet you the same way and you will have a hyperactive dog on your hands.

or crate is the key factor here. The area must be large enough so that the puppy can lie down and stretch out, as well as stand up, without rubbing his head on the top. At the same time, it must be small enough so that he cannot relieve himself at one end and sleep at the other without coming into contact with his droppings before he is fully trained to relieve

PAPER CAPER
Never line your pup's sleeping area with newspaper. Puppy litters are usually raised on newspaper and, once in your home, the puppy will immediately associate newspaper with voiding. Never put newspaper on any floor while house-training, as this will only confuse the puppy. If you are paper-training him, use paper in his designated relief area ONLY. Finally, restrict water intake after evening meals. Offer a few licks at a time—never let a young puppy gulp water after meals.

himself outside. Dogs are, by nature, clean animals and will not remain close to their relief areas unless forced to do so. In those cases, they then become dirty dogs and usually remain that way for life.

The dog's designated area should contain clean bedding and a toy. Water must always be available, in a non-spill container.

CONTROL
By control, we mean helping the puppy to create a lifestyle pattern that will be compatible to that of his human pack (YOU!). Just as we guide little children to learn our way of life, we must show the puppy when it is time to play, eat, sleep, exercise and even entertain himself.

Your puppy should always sleep in his crate. He should also

CANINE DEVELOPMENT SCHEDULE

It is important to understand how and at what age a puppy develops into adulthood. If you are a puppy owner, consult the following Canine Development Schedule to determine the stage of development your puppy is currently experiencing. This knowledge will help you as you work with the puppy in the weeks and months ahead.

Period	Age	Characteristics
FIRST TO THIRD	BIRTH TO SEVEN WEEKS	Puppy needs food, sleep and warmth, and responds to simple and gentle touching. Needs mother for security and disciplining. Needs littermates for learning and interacting with other dogs. Pup learns to function within a pack and learns pack order of dominance. Begin socialising with adults and children for short periods. Begins to become aware of its environment.
FOURTH	EIGHT TO TWELVE WEEKS	Brain is fully developed. Needs socialising with outside world. Remove from mother and littermates. Needs to change from canine pack to human pack. Human dominance necessary. Fear period occurs between 8 and 12 weeks. Avoid fright and pain.
FIFTH	THIRTEEN TO SIXTEEN WEEKS	Training and formal obedience should begin. Less association with other dogs, more with people, places, situations. Period will pass easily if you remember this is pup's change-to-adolescence time. Be firm and fair. Flight instinct prominent. Permissiveness and over-disciplining can do permanent damage. Praise for good behaviour.
JUVENILE	FOUR TO EIGHT MONTHS	Another fear period about 7 to 8 months of age. It passes quickly, but be cautious of fright and pain. Sexual maturity reached. Dominant traits established. Dog should understand sit, down, come and stay by now.

NOTE: THESE ARE APPROXIMATE TIME FRAMES. ALLOW FOR INDIVIDUAL DIFFERENCES IN PUPPIES.

learn that, during times of household confusion and excessive human activity, such as at breakfast when family members are preparing for the day, he can play by himself in relative safety and comfort in his designated area. Each time you leave the puppy alone, he should understand exactly where he is to stay.

Puppies are chewers. They cannot tell the difference between

HOW MANY TIMES A DAY?

AGE	RELIEF TRIPS
To 14 weeks	10
14–22 weeks	8
22–32 weeks	6
Adulthood	4
(dog stops growing)	

These are estimates, of course, but they are a guide to the MINIMUM opportunities a dog should have each day to relieve himself.

lamp cords, television wires, shoes, table legs, etc. Chewing into a television wire, for example, can be fatal to the puppy, while a shorted wire can start a fire in the house. If the puppy chews on the arm of the chair when he is alone, you will probably discipline him angrily when you get home. Thus, he makes the association that your coming home means he is going to be punished. (He will not remember chewing the chair and is incapable of making the association of the discipline with his naughty deed.) Accustoming the pup to his designated area not only keeps him safe but also avoids his engaging in destructive behaviours when you are not around.

Times of excitement, such as special occasions, family parties, etc., can be fun for the puppy providing that he can view the activities from the security of his designated area. He is not underfoot and he is not being fed all sorts of titbits that will probably cause him stomach distress, yet he still feels a part of the fun.

SCHEDULE

A puppy should be taken to his relief area each time he is released from his designated area, after meals, after a play session and when he first awakens in the morning (at age eight weeks, this can mean 5 a.m.!). The puppy will indicate that he's ready 'to go' by circling or sniffing busily—do not misinterpret these signs. For a puppy less than ten weeks of age, a routine of taking him out every hour is necessary. As the puppy grows, he will be able to wait for

THE SUCCESS METHOD

6 Steps to Successful Crate Training

1 Tell the puppy 'Crate time!' and place him in the crate with a small treat (a piece of cheese or half of a biscuit). Let him stay in the crate for five minutes while you are in the same room. Then release him and praise lavishly. Never release him when he is fussing. Wait until he is quiet before you let him out.

2 Repeat Step 1 several times a day.

3 The next day, place the puppy in the crate as before. Let him stay there for ten minutes. Do this several times.

4 Continue building time in five-minute increments until the puppy stays in his crate for 30 minutes with you in the room. Always take him to his relief area after prolonged periods in his crate.

5 Now go back to Step 1 and let the puppy stay in his crate for five minutes, this time while you are out of the room.

6 Once again, build crate time in five-minute increments with you out of the room. When the puppy will stay willingly in his crate (he may even fall asleep!) for 30 minutes with you out of the room, he will be ready to stay in it for several hours at a time.

HOUSE-TRAINING TIP
Most of all, be consistent. Always take your dog to the same location, always use the same command and always have the dog on lead when he is in his relief area, unless a fenced-in garden is available.

By following the Success Method, your puppy will be completely house-trained by the time his muscle and brain development reach maturity. Keep in mind that small breeds usually mature faster than large breeds, but all puppies should be trained by six months of age.

THE GOLDEN RULE
The golden rule of dog training is simple. For each 'question' (command), there is only one correct answer (reaction). One command = one reaction. Keep practising the command until the dog reacts correctly without hesitating. Be repetitive but not monotonous. Dogs get bored just as people do!

Do not carry your Spinone to his relief area. Lead him there or call him to follow you.

return to his relief area. Wait a few minutes, then return to the house again. Never hit a puppy or rub his face in urine or excrement when he has had an accident!

Once indoors, put the puppy in his crate until you have had time to clean up his accident. Then, release him to the family area and watch him more closely than before. Chances are, his accident was a result of your not picking up his signal or waiting too long before offering him the

longer periods of time.

Keep trips to his relief area short. Stay no more than five or six minutes and then return to the house. If he goes during that time, praise him lavishly and take him indoors immediately. If he does not, but he has an accident when you go back indoors, pick him up immediately, say 'No! No!' and

opportunity to relieve himself. Never hold a grudge against the puppy for accidents.

Let the puppy learn that going outdoors means it is time to relieve himself, not to play. Once trained, he will be able to play indoors and out and still differentiate between the times for play versus the times for relief.

Help him develop regular hours for naps, being alone, playing by himself and just resting, all in his crate. Encourage him to entertain himself while you are busy with your activities. Let him learn that having you near is comforting, but it is not your main purpose in life to provide him with undivided attention.

Each time you put your puppy in his own area, use the same command, whatever suits best. Soon he will run to his crate or special area when he hears you say those words.

Crate training provides safety for you, the puppy and the home. It also provides the puppy with a feeling of security, and that helps the puppy achieve self-confidence and clean habits. Remember that one of the primary ingredients in house-training your puppy is control. Regardless of your lifestyle, there will always be occasions when you will need to have a place where your dog can stay and be happy and safe. Crate training is the answer for now and

TAKE THE LEAD
Do not carry your dog to his toilet area. Lead him there on a leash or, better yet, encourage him to follow you to the spot. If you start carrying him to his spot, you might end up doing this routine forever and your dog will have the satisfaction of having trained YOU.

in the future.

In conclusion, a few key elements are really all you need for a successful house-training method—consistency, frequency, praise, control and supervision. By following these procedures with a normal, healthy puppy, you and the puppy will soon be past the stage of accidents and ready to move on to a full and rewarding life together.

ROLES OF DISCIPLINE, REWARD AND PUNISHMENT
Discipline, training one to act in accordance with rules, brings order to life. It is as simple as

that. Without discipline, particularly in a group society, chaos will reign supreme and the group will eventually perish. Humans and canines are social animals and need some form of discipline in order to function effectively. They must procure food, protect their home base and their young and reproduce to keep their species going. If there were no discipline in the lives of social animals, they would eventually die from starvation and/or predation by other stronger animals.

In the case of domestic canines, discipline in their lives is needed in order for them to understand how their pack (you and other family members) functions and how they must act in order to survive.

A large humane society in a highly populated area recently surveyed dog owners regarding their satisfaction with their relationships with their dogs. People who had trained their dogs were 75% more satisfied with their pets than those who had never trained their dogs.

Dr Edward Thorndike, a psychologist, established *Thorndike's Theory of Learning*, which states that a behaviour that results in a pleasant event tends to be repeated. A behaviour that results in an unpleasant event tends not to be repeated. It is this theory upon which training methods are based today. For example, if you manipulate a dog to perform a specific behaviour and reward him for doing it, he is likely to do it again because he enjoyed the end result.

Occasionally, punishment, a penalty inflicted for an offence, is necessary. The best type of punishment often comes from an outside source. For example, a

PRACTICE MAKES PERFECT!
• Have training lessons with your dog every day in several short segments—three to five times a day for a few minutes at a time is ideal.
• Do not have long practice sessions. The dog will become easily bored.
• Never practise when you are tired, ill, worried or in an otherwise negative mood. This will transmit to the dog and may have an adverse effect on his performance.

Think fun, short and above all POSITIVE! End each session on a high note, rather than a failed exercise, and make sure to give a lot of praise. Enjoy the training and help your dog enjoy it, too.

THE HAND THAT FEEDS

To a dog's way of thinking, your hands are like his mouth in terms of a defence mechanism. If you squeeze him too tightly, he might just bite you because that would be his normal response. This is not aggressive biting and, although all biting should be discouraged, you need the discipline in learning how to handle your dog.

child is told not to touch the stove because he may get burned. He disobeys and touches the stove. In doing so, he receives a burn. From that time on, he respects the heat of the stove and avoids contact with it. Therefore, a behaviour that results in an unpleasant event tends not to be repeated.

A good example of a dog learning the hard way is the dog who chases the house cat. He is told many times to leave the cat

'NO' MEANS 'NO!'

Dogs do not understand our language. They can be trained to react to a certain sound, at a certain volume. If you say 'No, Oliver' in a very soft pleasant voice it will not have the same meaning as 'No, Oliver!!' when you shout it as loud as you can. You should never use the dog's name during a reprimand, just the command NO!!

alone, yet he persists in teasing the cat. Then, one day, the dog begins chasing the cat but the cat turns and swipes a claw across the dog's face, leaving the dog with a painful gash on his nose. The final result is that the dog stops chasing the cat. Again, a behaviour that results in an unpleasant event tends not to be repeated.

TRAINING EQUIPMENT

COLLAR AND LEAD
For a Spinone, the collar and lead that you use for training must be one with which you are easily able to work, not too heavy for the dog and perfectly safe.

TREATS
Have a bag of treats on hand; something nutritious and easy to swallow works best. Use a soft treat, a chunk of cheese or a piece of cooked chicken rather than a dry biscuit. By the time the dog has finished chewing a dry treat, he will forget why he is being rewarded in the first place!

Using food rewards will not teach a dog to beg at the table—the only way to teach a dog to beg at the table is to give him food from the table. In training, rewarding the dog with a food treat will help him associate praise and the treats with learning new behaviours that obviously please his owner.

TRAINING BEGINS: ASK THE DOG A QUESTION

In order to teach your dog anything, you must first get his attention. After all, he cannot learn anything if he is looking away from you with his mind on something else.

To get your dog's attention, ask him 'School?' and immediately walk over to him and give him a treat as you tell him 'Good dog.' Wait a minute or two and

Training includes teaching and enforcing the house rules; for example, will the pup be allowed on the furniture?

repeat the routine, this time with a treat in your hand as you approach within a foot of the dog. Do not go directly to him, but stop about a foot short of him and hold out the treat as you ask 'School?' He will see you approaching with a treat in your hand and most likely begin walking toward you. As you meet, give him the treat and praise again.

The third time, ask the

> ### OPEN MINDS
> Dogs are as different from each other as people are. What works for one dog may not work for another. Have an open mind. If one method of training is unsuccessful, try another.

question, have a treat in your hand and walk only a short distance toward the dog so that he must walk almost all the way to you. As he reaches you, give him the treat and praise again.

By this time, the dog will probably be getting the idea that if he pays attention to you, especially when you ask that question, it will pay off in treats and enjoyable activities for him. In other words, he learns that 'school' means doing great things with you that are fun and that result in positive attention for him.

> ### TRAINING RULES
> If you want to be successful in training your dog, you have four rules to obey yourself:
> 1. Develop an understanding of how a dog thinks.
> 2. Do not blame the dog for lack of communication.
> 3. Define your dog's personality and act accordingly.
> 4. Have patience and be consistent.

Remember that the dog does not understand your verbal language; he only recognises sounds. Your question translates to a series of sounds for him, and those sounds become the signal to go to you and pay attention. The dog learns that if he does this, he will get to interact with you plus receive treats and praise.

THE BASIC COMMANDS

TEACHING SIT

Now that you have the dog's attention, attach his lead and hold it in your left hand, and hold a food treat in your right hand. Place your food hand at the dog's nose and let him lick the treat but not take it from you. Say 'Sit' and slowly raise your food hand from in front of the dog's nose up over his head so that he is looking at the ceiling. As he bends his head upward, he will have to bend his knees to maintain his balance. As he bends his knees, he will assume a sit position. At that point, release the food treat and praise lavishly with comments such as 'Good dog! Good sit!,' etc. Remember to always praise enthusiastically, because dogs relish verbal praise from their owners and feel so proud of themselves whenever they accomplish a behaviour.

You will not use food forever in getting the dog to obey your commands. Food is only used to teach new behaviours and, once the dog knows what you want when you give a specific command, you will wean him off the food treats but still maintain the verbal praise. After all, you will always have your voice with you, and there will be many times when you have no food rewards but expect the dog to obey.

A basic command is the sit exercise. It is simple to teach and the dog usually learns the command quickly.

DOUBLE JEOPARDY
A dog in jeopardy never lies down. He stays alert on his feet because instinct tells him that he may have to run away or fight for his survival. Therefore, if a dog feels threatened or anxious, he will not lie down. Consequently, it is important to have the dog calm and relaxed as he learns the down exercise.

You can teach your Spinone to stay in the sit, down or standing position. Once the dog has mastered the stay, you can practise the command without the lead.

TEACHING DOWN

Teaching the down exercise is easy when you understand how the dog perceives the down position, and it is very difficult when you do not. Dogs perceive the down position as a submissive one; therefore, teaching the down exercise by using a forceful method can sometimes make the dog develop such a fear of the down that he either runs away when you say 'Down' or he attempts to snap at the person who tries to force him down.

Have the dog sit close alongside your left leg, facing in the same direction as you are. Hold the lead in your left hand and a food treat in your right. Now place your left hand lightly on the top of the dog's shoulders where they meet above the spinal cord. Do not push down on the dog's shoulders; simply rest your left hand there so you can guide the dog to lie down close to your left leg rather than to swing away from your side when he drops.

Now place the food hand at the dog's nose, say 'Down' very softly (almost a whisper), and slowly lower the food hand to the dog's front feet. When the food hand reaches the floor,

begin moving it forward along the floor in front of the dog. Keep talking softly to the dog, saying things like, 'Do you want this treat? You can do this, good dog.' Your reassuring tone of voice will help calm the dog as he tries to follow the food hand in order to get the treat.

When the dog's elbows touch the floor, release the food and praise softly. Try to get the dog to maintain that down position for several seconds before you let him sit up again. The goal here is to get the dog to settle down and not feel threatened in the down position.

PLAN TO PLAY
The puppy should also have regular play and exercise sessions when he is with you or a family member. Exercise for a very young puppy can consist of a short walk around the house or garden. Playing can include fetching games with a large ball or a special raggy. (All puppies teethe and need soft things upon which to chew.) Remember to restrict play periods to indoors within his living area (the family room, for example) until he is completely house-trained.

TEACHING STAY

It is easy to teach the dog to stay in either a sit or a down position. Again, we use food and praise during the teaching process as we help the dog to understand exactly what it is that we are expecting him to do.

To teach the sit/stay, start with the dog sitting on your left side as before and hold the lead in your left hand. Have a food treat in your right hand and place your food hand at the dog's nose. Say 'Stay' and step out on your right foot to stand directly in front of the dog, toe to toe, as he licks and nibbles the treat. Be sure to keep his head facing upward to maintain the sit position. Count to five and then swing around to stand next to the dog again with him on your left. As soon as you get back to the original position, release the food and praise lavishly.

To teach the down/stay, do the down as previously described. As

CONSISTENCY PAYS OFF

Dogs need consistency in their feeding schedule, exercise and toilet breaks, and in the verbal commands you use. If you use 'Stay' on Monday and 'Stay here, please' on Tuesday, you will confuse your dog. Don't demand perfect behaviour during training classes and then let him have the run of the house the rest of the day. Above all, lavish praise on your pet consistently every time he does something right. The more he feels he is pleasing you, the more willing he will be to learn.

FEAR AGGRESSION

Pups who are subjected to physical abuse during training commonly end up with behavioural problems as adults. One common result of abuse is fear aggression, in which a dog will lash out, bare his teeth, snarl and finally bite someone by whom he feels threatened. For example, your daughter may be playing with the dog one afternoon. As they play hide-and-seek, she backs the dog into a corner and, as she attempts to tease him playfully, he bites her hand. Examine the cause of this behaviour. Did your daughter ever hit the dog? Did someone who resembles your daughter hit or scream at the dog?

Fortunately, fear aggression is relatively easy to correct. Have your daughter engage in only positive activities with the dog, such as feeding, petting and walking. She should not give any corrections or negative feedback. If the dog still growls or cowers away from her, allow someone else to accompany them. After approximately one week, the dog should feel that he can rely on her for many positive things, and he will also be prevented from reacting fearfully towards anyone who might resemble her.

SAFETY FIRST

While it may seem that the most important things to your dog are eating, sleeping and chewing the upholstery on your furniture, his first concern is actually safety. The domesticated dogs we keep as companions have the same pack instinct as their ancestors who ran free thousands of years ago. Because of this pack instinct, your dog wants to know that he and his pack are not in danger of being harmed, and that his pack has a strong, capable leader. You must establish yourself as the leader early on in your relationship. That way your dog will trust that you will take care of him and the pack, and he will accept your commands without question.

food will not be touching the dog's nose. He will watch the food hand and quickly learn that he is going to get that treat as soon as you return to his side.

When you can stand 1 metre away from your dog for 30 seconds, you can then begin building time and distance in both stays. Eventually, the dog can be expected to remain in the stay position for prolonged periods of time until you return to him or call him to you. Always praise lavishly when he stays.

soon as the dog lies down, say 'Stay' and step out on your right foot just as you did in the sit/stay. Count to five and then return to stand beside the dog with him on your left side. Release the treat and praise as always.

Within a week or ten days, you can begin to add a bit of distance between you and your dog when you leave him. When you do, use your left hand open with the palm facing the dog as a stay signal, much the same as the hand signal a constable uses to stop traffic at an intersection. Hold the food treat in your right hand as before, but this time the

FAMILY TIES

If you have other pets in the home and/or interact often with the pets of friends and other family members, your pup will respond to those pets in much the same manner as you do. It is only when you show fear of or resentment toward another animal that he will act fearful or unfriendly.

'Where are you?' will get your dog's attention and make him want to come to you.

TEACHING COME

If you make teaching 'come' an exciting experience, you should never have a student that does not love the game or that fails to come when called. The secret, it seems, is never to teach the word 'come.'

At times when an owner most wants his dog to come when called, the owner is likely to be upset or anxious and he allows these feelings to come through in the tone of his voice when he calls his dog. Hearing that desperation in his owner's voice, the dog fears the results of going to him and therefore either disobeys outright or runs in the opposite direction. The secret, therefore, is to teach the dog a game and, when you want him to come to you, simply play the game. It is practically a no-fail solution!

To begin, have several members of your family take a few food treats and each go into a different room in the house. Everyone takes turns calling the dog, and each person should celebrate the dog's finding him with a treat and lots of happy praise. When a person calls the dog, he is actually inviting the dog to find him and to get a treat as a reward for 'winning.'

A few turns of the 'Where are you?' game and the dog will understand that everyone is playing the game and that each person has a big celebration awaiting the dog's success at locating him or her. Once the dog learns to love the game, simply calling out 'Where are you?' will bring him running from wherever he is when he hears that all-important question.

'COME' . . . BACK

Never call your dog to come to you for a correction or scold him when he reaches you. That is the quickest way to turn a 'Come' command into 'Go away fast!' Dogs think only in the present tense, and your dog will connect the scolding with coming to you, not with the misbehaviour of a few moments earlier.

The come command is recognised as one of the most important things to teach a dog, but there are trainers who work with thousands of dogs and never teach the actual word 'Come.' Yet these dogs will race to respond to a person who uses the dog's name followed by 'Where are you?' For example, a woman has a 12-year-old companion dog who went blind, but who never fails to locate her owner when asked, 'Where are you?'

Children, in particular, love to play this game with their dogs. Children can hide in smaller places like a shower or bath, behind a bed or under a table. The dog needs to work a little bit harder to find these hiding places, but, when he does, he loves to celebrate with a treat and a tussle with a favourite youngster.

TEACHING HEEL

Heeling means that the dog walks beside the owner without pulling. It takes time and patience on the owner's part to succeed at teaching the dog that he (the owner) will not proceed unless the dog is walking calmly beside him. Neither pulling out ahead on the lead nor lagging behind is acceptable.

Begin by holding the lead in your left hand as the dog sits beside your left leg. Move the loop end of the lead to your right hand, but keep your left hand

short on the lead so that it keeps the dog in close next to you.

Say 'Heel' and step forward on your left foot. Keep the dog close to you and take three steps. Stop and have the dog sit next to you in what we now call the 'heel position.' Praise verbally, but do not touch the dog. Hesitate a moment and begin again with 'Heel,' taking three steps and stopping, at which point the dog is told to sit again.

Your goal here is to have the dog walk those three steps

THE STUDENT'S STRESS TEST

During training sessions you must be able to recognise signs of stress in your dog such as:
- tucking his tail between his legs
- lowering his head
- shivering or trembling
- standing completely still or running away
- panting and/or salivating
- avoiding eye contact
- flattening his ears back
- urinating submissively
- rolling over and lifting a leg
- grinning or baring teeth
- aggression when restrained

If your four-legged student displays these signs, he may just be nervous or intimidated. The training session may have been too lengthy, with not enough praise and affirmation. Stop for the day and try again tomorrow.

without pulling on the lead. Once he will walk calmly beside you for three steps without pulling, increase the number of steps you take to five. When he will walk politely beside you while you take five steps, you can increase the length of your walk to ten steps. Keep increasing the length of your stroll until the dog will walk quietly beside you without pulling as long as you want him to heel. When you stop heeling, indicate to the dog that the exercise is over by verbally

A Spinone heels in the show ring as his gait is evaluated. Learning to heel is necessary for all dogs, not just show dogs.

HEELING WELL

Teach your dog to heel in an enclosed area. Once you think the dog will obey reliably and you want to attempt advanced obedience exercises such as off-lead heeling, test him in a fenced-in area so he cannot run away.

praising as you pet him and say 'OK, good dog.' The 'OK' is used as a release word, meaning that the exercise is finished and the dog is free to relax.

If you are dealing with a dog who insists on pulling you around, simply 'put on your brakes' and stand your ground until the dog realises that the two of you are not going anywhere until he is beside you and moving at your pace, not his. It may take some time just standing there to convince the dog that you are the leader and that you will be the one to decide on the direction and speed of your travel.

Each time the dog looks up at you or slows down to give a slack lead between the two of you,

TRAINING TIP

If you are walking your dog and he suddenly stops and looks straight into your eyes, ignore him. Pull the leash and lead him into the direction you want to walk.

TUG OF WALK?

If you begin teaching the heel by taking long walks and letting the dog pull you along, he misinterprets this action as an acceptable form of taking a walk. When you pull back on the lead to counteract his pulling, he reads that tug as a signal to pull even harder!

COMMAND STANCE

Stand up straight and authoritatively when giving your dog commands. Do not issue commands when lying on the floor or lying on your back on the sofa. If you are on your hands and knees when you give a command, your dog will think you are positioning yourself to play.

quietly praise him and say, 'Good heel. Good dog.' Eventually, the dog will begin to respond and within a few days he will be walking politely beside you without pulling on the lead. At first, the training sessions should be kept short and very positive; soon the dog will be able to walk nicely with you for increasingly longer distances. Remember also to give the dog free time and the opportunity to run and play when you have finished heel practice.

WEANING OFF FOOD IN TRAINING

Food is used in training new behaviours. Once the dog understands what behaviour goes with a specific command, it is time to start weaning him off the food treats. At first, give a treat after each exercise. Then,

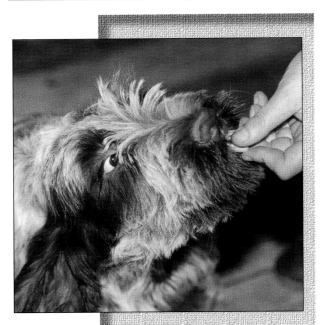

HOW TO WEAN THE 'TREAT HOG'

If you have trained your dog by rewarding him with a treat each time he performs a command, he may soon decide that without the treat, he won't sit, stay or come. The best way to fix this problem is to start asking your dog to do certain commands twice before being rewarded. Slowly increase the number of commands given and then vary the number: three sits and a treat one day, five sits for a biscuit the next day, etc. Your dog will soon realise that there is no set number of sits before he gets his reward, and he'll likely do it the first time you ask in the hope of being rewarded sooner rather than later.

start to give a treat only after every other exercise. Mix up the times when you offer a food reward and the times when you only offer praise so that the dog will never know when he is going to receive both food and praise and when he is going to receive only praise. This is called a variable ratio reward system. It proves successful because there is always the chance that the owner will produce a treat, so the dog never stops trying for that reward. No matter what, ALWAYS give verbal praise.

OBEDIENCE CLASSES

It is a good idea to enrol in an obedience class if one is available in your area. If yours is a show dog, ringcraft classes would be

DID YOU KNOW?

Occasionally, a dog and owner who have not attended formal classes have been able to earn entry-level titles by obtaining competition rules and regulations from a local kennel club and practising on their own to a degree of perfection. Obtaining the higher level titles, however, almost always requires extensive training under the tutelage of experienced instructors. In addition, the more difficult levels require more specialised equipment whereas the lower levels do not.

OBEDIENCE SCHOOL

A basic obedience beginner's class usually lasts for six to eight weeks. Dog and owner attend an hour-long lesson once a week and practise for a few minutes, several times a day, each day at home. If done properly, the whole procedure will result in a well-mannered dog and an owner who delights in living with a pet that is eager to please and enjoys doing things with his owner.

more appropriate. Many areas have dog clubs that offer basic obedience training as well as preparatory classes for obedience competition. There are also local dog trainers who offer similar classes.

At obedience shows, dogs can earn titles at various levels of competition. The beginning levels of obedience competition include basic behaviours such as sit, down, heel, etc. The more advanced levels of competition

OBEDIENCE SCHOOL

Taking your dog to an obedience school may be the best investment in time and money you can ever make. You will enjoy the benefits for the lifetime of your dog and you will have the opportunity to meet people who have similar expectations for their companion dogs.

include jumping, retrieving, scent discrimination and signal work. The advanced levels require a dog and owner to put a lot of time and effort into their training. The titles that can be earned at these levels of competition are very prestigious.

OTHER ACTIVITIES FOR LIFE

Whether a dog is trained in the structured environment of a class or alone with his owner at home, there are many activities that can bring fun and rewards to both owner and dog once they have mastered basic control.

Teaching the dog to help out around the home, in the garden or on the farm provides great satisfaction to both dog and owner. In addition, the dog's help makes life a little easier for his owner and raises his stature as a valued companion to his family. It helps give the dog a purpose by occupying his mind and providing an outlet for his energy.

Backpacking is an exciting and healthy activity that the dog can be taught without assistance from more than his owner. The exercise of walking and climbing is good for man and dog alike, and the bond that they develop together is priceless. The rule for backpacking with any dog is never to expect the dog to carry more than one-sixth of his body weight.

If you are interested in participating in organised competition with your Spinone, there are activities other than obedience in which you and your dog can become involved. The most obvious of these for the Spinone owner are field trials, organised outings that test the breed's natural hunting ability. Field trials are not designed for the casual participant, as the sport requires significant investment of time, talent, effort and money.

Retriever training in progress! Spinoni love activities that utilise their natural abilities and energy.

You can find out more about field trials by contacting The Kennel Club or your national Italian Spinone club.

Agility is a popular sport in which dogs run through an obstacle course that includes various jumps, tunnels and other exercises to test the dog's speed and co-ordination. The owners run beside their dogs to give commands and to guide them through the course. Although competitive, the focus is on fun—it's fun to do, fun to watch and great exercise.

Whatever activities and sports you decide to undertake with your Italian Spinone, you will certainly be glad that you invested the time to train him properly. From the basics of obedience to the rigorous education of competitive trials, the Spinone is a gifted student who wants nothing more than to delight his master.

The water retrieve: (top) The Spinone swims out to the bird, which has been shot over the water. (bottom) The Spinone holds the bird gently in his mouth while returning to shore.

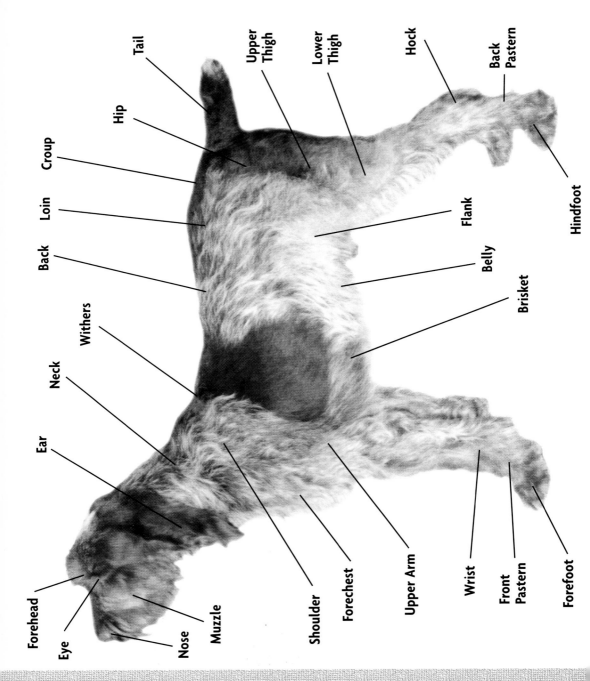

PHYSICAL STRUCTURE OF THE ITALIAN SPINONE

ITALIAN SPINONE

Dogs suffer from many of the same physical illnesses as people. They might even share many of the same psychological problems. Since people usually know more about human diseases than canine maladies, many of the terms used in this chapter will be familiar but not necessarily those used by veterinary surgeons. For example we will use the term *x-ray*, instead of the more acceptable term *radiograph*. We will also use the familiar term *symptoms* even though dogs don't have symptoms, which are verbal descriptions of the patient's feelings; dogs have *clinical signs*. Since dogs can't speak, we have to look for clinical signs...but we still use the term *symptoms* in this book.

As a general rule, medicine is *practised*. That term is not arbitrary. Medicine is a constantly changing art as we learn more and more about genetics, electronic aids (like CAT scans) and daily laboratory advances. There are many dog maladies, like canine hip dysplasia, which are not universally treated in the same manner. Some veterinary surgeons opt for surgery more often than others do.

SELECTING A VETERINARY SURGEON

Your selection of a veterinary surgeon should not be based upon personality (as most are) but upon his convenience to your home. You want a vet who is close because you might have emergencies or need to make multiple visits for treatments. You want a vet who has services that you might require such as tattooing and grooming, as well as sophisticated pet supplies and a good reputation for ability and responsiveness. There is nothing more frustrating than having to wait a day or more to get a response from your veterinary surgeon.

All veterinary surgeons are licensed and their diplomas and/or certificates should be displayed in their waiting rooms. There are, however, many veterinary specialities that usually require further studies and internships. There are specialists in heart problems (veterinary cardiologists), skin problems (veterinary dermatologists), teeth and gum problems (veterinary dentists), eye problems (veterinary ophthalmologists) and x-rays (veterinary radiologists), as well as vets who have specialities in

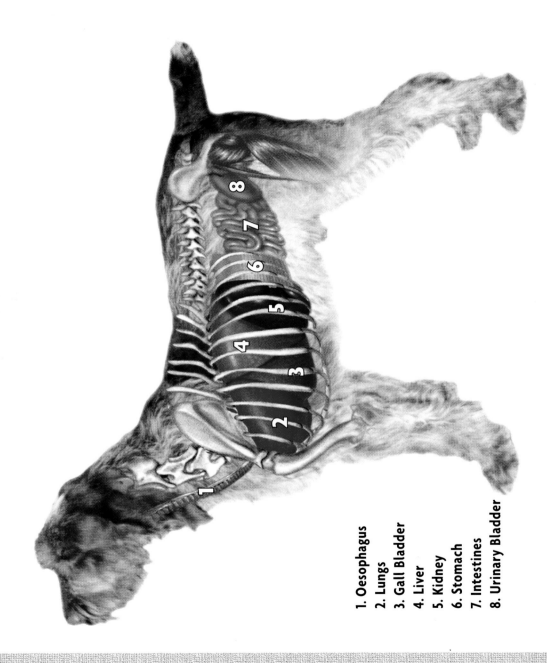

1. Oesophagus
2. Lungs
3. Gall Bladder
4. Liver
5. Kidney
6. Stomach
7. Intestines
8. Urinary Bladder

INTERNAL ORGANS OF THE ITALIAN SPINONE

bones, muscles or other organs. Most veterinary surgeons do routine surgery such as neutering, stitching up wounds and docking tails for those breeds in which such is required for show purposes.

When the problem affecting your dog is serious, it is not unusual or impudent to get another medical opinion, although in Britain you are obliged to advise the vets concerned about this. You might also want to compare costs among several veterinary surgeons. Sophisticated health care and veterinary services can be very costly. It is not infrequent that important decisions are based upon financial considerations.

PREVENTATIVE MEDICINE

It is much easier, less costly and more effective to practise preventative medicine than to fight bouts of illness and disease. Properly bred puppies come from parents who were selected based upon their genetic disease profiles. Their mothers should have been vaccinated, free of all internal and external parasites and properly nourished. The dam can pass on disease resistance to her puppies, which can last for eight to ten weeks, but she can also pass on parasites and many infections. For these reasons, a visit to the veterinary surgeon who cared for the dam is recommended.

Breakdown of Veterinary Income by Category

2%	Dentistry
4%	Radiology
12%	Surgery
15%	Vaccinations
19%	Laboratory
23%	Examinations
25%	Medicines

A typical American vet's income, categorised according to services performed. This survey dealt with small-animal (pets) practices.

VACCINATION SCHEDULING
Most vaccinations are given by injection and should only be done by a veterinary surgeon. Both he and you should keep records of the date of the injection, the identification of the vaccine and the amount given. Some vets give a first vaccination at eight weeks, but most dog breeders prefer the course not to commence until about ten weeks to avoid negating any antibodies passed on by the dam. The vaccination scheduling is usually based on a 15-day cycle. You must take your vet's advice regarding when to vaccinate, as this may differ according to the vaccine used. Most vaccinations immunize your puppy against viruses.

The usual vaccines contain immunizing doses of several

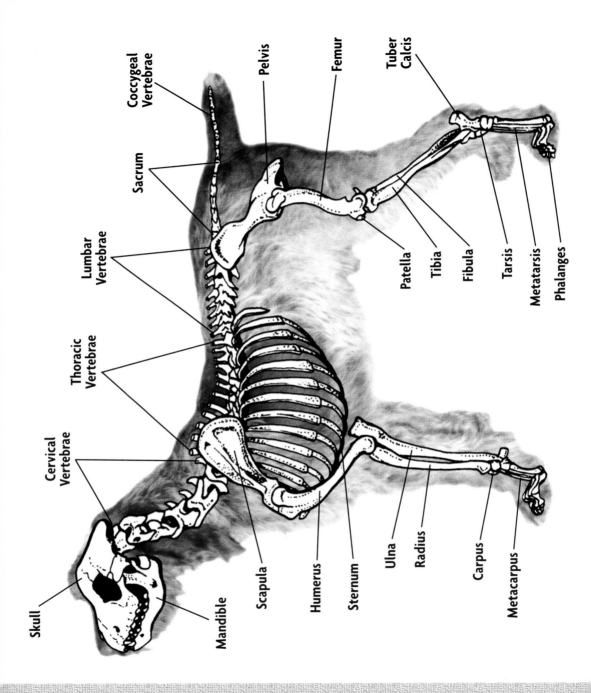

Coccygeal
Vertebrae

Pelvis

Femur

Tuber
Calcis

Sacrum

Lumbar
Vertebrae

Patella

Tibia

Fibula

Tarsis

Metatarsis

Phalanges

Thoracic
Vertebrae

Cervical
Vertebrae

Skull

Mandible

Scapula

Humerus

Sternum

Ulna

Radius

Carpus

Metacarpus

SKELETAL STRUCTURE OF THE ITALIAN SPINONE

different viruses such as distemper, parvovirus, parainfluenza and hepatitis, although some veterinary surgeons recommend separate vaccines for each disease. There are other vaccines available when the puppy is at risk. You should rely upon professional advice. This is especially true for the booster-shot programme. Most vaccination programmes require a booster when the puppy is a year old and once a year thereafter. In some cases, circumstances may require more or less frequent immunizations. Kennel cough, more formally known as tracheobronchitis, is treated with a vaccine that is sprayed into the dog's nostrils. Kennel cough is usually included in routine vaccination, but this is often not so effective as for other major diseases.

WEANING TO FIVE MONTHS OLD

Puppies should be weaned by the time they are about two months old. A puppy that remains for at least eight weeks with its mother and littermates usually adapts better to other dogs and people later in life. Some new owners have their puppies examined by veterinary surgeons immediately, which is a good idea. Vaccination programmes usually begin when the puppy is very young.

The puppy will have its teeth examined and have its skeletal conformation and general health checked prior to certification by the veterinary surgeon. Spinone puppies may have problems with their kneecaps, cataracts and other eye problems, heart murmurs or undescended testicles. They may also have personality problems, though this is uncommon with the Spinone, and your veterinary surgeon might have training in temperament evaluation.

FIVE TO TWELVE MONTHS OF AGE

Unless you intend to breed or show your dog, neutering the puppy at six months of age is recommended. Discuss this with your veterinary surgeon. Neutering has proven to be extremely beneficial to both male and female puppies. Besides eliminating the possibility of pregnancy, it inhibits (but does not prevent) breast cancer in bitches and prostate cancer in male dogs. Under no circumstances should a bitch be spayed prior to her first season.

Your veterinary surgeon should provide your puppy with a thorough dental evaluation at six months of age, ascertaining whether all the permanent teeth have erupted properly. A home dental care regimen should be initiated at six months, including brushing weekly and providing good dental devices (such as nylon bones). Regular dental care promotes healthy teeth, fresh breath and a longer life.

ONE TO SEVEN YEARS

Once a year, your grown dog should visit the vet for an examination and vaccination boosters, if needed. Some vets recommend blood tests, a thyroid-level check and a dental evaluation to accompany these annual visits. A thorough clinical evaluation by the vet can provide critical background information for your dog. Blood tests are often performed at one year of age, and dental examinations around the third or fourth birthday. In the long run, quality preventative care for your pet can save money, teeth and lives.

SKIN PROBLEMS IN SPINONI

Veterinary surgeons are consulted by dog owners for skin problems more than for any other group of diseases or maladies. Dogs' skin is almost as sensitive as human skin, and both suffer from almost the same ailments (though the occurrence of acne in dogs is rare!). For this reason, veterinary dermatology

DISEASE REFERENCE CHART

	What is it?	What causes it?	Symptoms
Leptospirosis	Severe disease that affects the internal organs; can be spread to people.	A bacterium, which is often carried by rodents, that enters through mucous membranes and spreads quickly throughout the body.	Range from fever, vomiting and loss of appetite in less severe cases to shock, irreversible kidney damage and possibly death in most severe cases.
Rabies	Potentially deadly virus that infects warm-blooded mammals. Not seen in United Kingdom.	Bite from a carrier of the virus, mainly wild animals.	1st stage: dog exhibits change in behaviour, fear. 2nd stage: dog's behaviour becomes more aggressive. 3rd stage: loss of coordination, trouble with bodily functions.
Parvovirus	Highly contagious virus, potentially deadly.	Ingestion of the virus, which is usually spread through the faeces of infected dogs.	Most common: severe diarrhoea. Also vomiting, fatigue, lack of appetite.
Kennel cough	Contagious respiratory infection.	Combination of types of bacteria and virus. Most common: *Bordetella bronchiseptica* bacteria and parainfluenza virus.	Chronic cough.
Distemper	Disease primarily affecting respiratory and nervous system.	Virus that is related to the human measles virus.	Mild symptoms such as fever, lack of appetite and mucous secretion progress to evidence of brain damage, 'hard pad.'
Hepatitis	Virus primarily affecting the liver.	Canine adenovirus type I (CAV-1). Enters system when dog breathes in particles.	Lesser symptoms include listlessness, diarrhoea, vomiting. More severe symptoms include 'blue-eye' (clumps of virus in eye).
Coronavirus	Virus resulting in digestive problems.	Virus is spread through infected dog's faeces.	Stomach upset evidenced by lack of appetite, vomiting, diarrhoea.

HEALTH AND VACCINATION SCHEDULE

AGE IN WEEKS:	6TH	8TH	10TH	12TH	14TH	16TH	20-24TH	1 YR
Worm Control	✔	✔	✔	✔	✔	✔	✔	
Neutering								✔
Heartworm		✔		✔		✔	✔	
Parvovirus	✔		✔		✔		✔	✔
Distemper		✔		✔		✔		✔
Hepatitis		✔		✔		✔		✔
Leptospirosis								✔
Parainfluenza	✔		✔		✔			✔
Dental Examination		✔					✔	✔
Complete Physical		✔					✔	✔
Coronavirus				✔			✔	✔
Kennel Cough	✔							
Hip Dysplasia								✔
Rabies							✔	

Vaccinations are not instantly effective. It takes about two weeks for the dog's immune system to develop antibodies. Most vaccinations require annual booster shots. Your veterinary surgeon should guide you in this regard.

has developed into a speciality practised by many veterinary surgeons.

Since many skin problems have visual symptoms that are almost identical, it requires the skill of an experienced veterinary dermatologist to identify and cure many of the more severe skin disorders. Pet shops sell many treatments for skin problems, but most of the treatments are directed at the symptoms and not the underlying problem(s). If your dog is suffering from a skin disorder, you should seek professional assistance as quickly as possible. As with all diseases, the earlier a problem is identified and treated, the more successful is the cure.

HEREDITARY SKIN DISORDERS
Veterinary dermatologists are currently researching a number of skin disorders that are believed to have an hereditary basis. These inherited diseases are transmitted by both parents,

PUPPY VACCINATIONS
Your veterinary surgeon will probably recommend that your puppy be vaccinated before you take him outside. There are airborne diseases, parasite eggs in the grass and unexpected visits from other dogs that might be dangerous to your puppy's health.

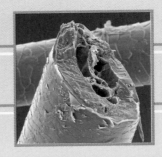

Normal hairs of a dog enlarged 200 times original size. The cuticle (outer covering) is clean and healthy. Unlike human hair that grows from the base, a dog's hair also grows from the end. Damaged hairs and split ends, illustrated above.

who appear (phenotypically) normal but have a recessive gene for the disease, meaning that they carry, but are not affected by, the disease. These diseases pose serious problems to breeders because in some instances there are no methods of identifying carriers. Often the secondary diseases associated with these skin conditions are even more debilitating than the skin disorders themselves, including cancers and respiratory problems; others can be lethal.

Among the hereditary skin disorders, for which the mode of inheritance is known, are acrodermatitis, cutaneous asthenia (Ehlers-Danlos syndrome), sebaceous adenitis, cyclic hematopoiesis, dermatomyositis, IgA deficiency, colour dilution alopaecia and nodular dermatofibrosis. Some of these disorders are limited to one or two breeds, while others affect a large number of breeds. All inherited diseases must be diagnosed and treated by a veterinary specialist.

PARASITE BITES

Many of us are allergic to insect bites. The bites itch, erupt and may even become infected. Dogs have the same reaction to fleas, ticks and/or mites. When an insect lands on you, you have the chance to whisk it away with your hand. Unfortunately, when your dog is bitten by a flea, tick or mite, he can only scratch it away or bite it. By the time the dog has been bitten, the parasite has done some of its damage. It may also have laid eggs, which will cause further problems in the near future. The itching from parasite bites is probably due to the saliva injected into the site when the parasite sucks the dog's blood.

AUTO-IMMUNE SKIN CONDITIONS

An auto-immune skin condition is commonly referred to as a condition in which a person (or dog) is 'allergic' to him- or herself, while an allergy is usually an inflammatory reaction to an outside stimulus. Auto-immune diseases cause serious damage to the tissues that are involved.

The best known auto-immune disease is lupus, which affects people as well as dogs. The symptoms are variable and may affect the kidneys, bones, blood chemistry and skin. It can be fatal to both dogs and humans, though it is not thought to be transmissible. It is usually successfully treated with cortisone, prednisone or a similar corticosteroid, but extensive use of these drugs can have harmful side effects.

ACRAL LICK GRANULOMA

Many large dogs have a very poorly understood syndrome called acral lick granuloma. The manifestation of the problem is the dog's tireless attack at a specific area of the body, almost always the legs or paws. The dog licks so intensively that he removes the hair and skin, leaving an ugly, large wound. Tiny protuberances, which are outgrowths of new capillaries, bead on the surface of the wound. Owners who notice their dogs' biting and chewing at their extremities should have the vet determine the cause. If lick granuloma is identified, although there is no absolute cure, corticosteroids are the most common treatment.

AIRBORNE ALLERGIES

An interesting allergy is pollen allergy. Humans have hay fever, rose fever and other fevers from which they suffer during the pollinating season. Many dogs suffer the same allergies. When the pollen count is high, your dog might suffer, but don't expect him to sneeze and have a runny nose as a human would. Dogs react to pollen allergies the same way they react to fleas—they scratch and bite themselves.

Dogs, like humans, can be tested for allergens. Discuss the testing with your veterinary dermatologist.

FOOD PROBLEMS

FOOD ALLERGIES

Dogs are allergic to many foods that are best-sellers and highly recommended by breeders and veterinary surgeons. Changing the brand of food that you buy may not eliminate the problem if the element to which the dog is allergic is contained in the new brand.

Recognising a food allergy is difficult. Humans vomit or have rashes when they eat a food to which they are allergic. Dogs neither vomit nor (usually) develop rashes. They react in the same manner as they would to an airborne or flea allergy; they itch, scratch and bite, thus making the diagnosis extremely difficult. While pollen allergies and parasite bites are usually seasonal, food allergies are year-round problems.

FOOD INTOLERANCE

Food intolerance is the inability of the dog to completely digest certain foods. One example are puppies that may have done very well on their mother's milk, but may not do well on cow's milk. The results of food intolerance may be evident in loose bowels, passing gas and stomach pains. These are the only obvious symptoms of food intolerance, which makes diagnosis difficult.

TREATING FOOD PROBLEMS

It is possible to handle food allergies and food intolerance yourself. Start by putting your dog on a diet that he has never had. Obviously, if the dog has never eaten this new food, he can't have been allergic or intolerant of it. Start with a single ingredient that is not in the dog's diet at the present time. Ingredients like chopped beef or fish are common in dogs' diets, so try something more exotic like rabbit, pheasant or even just vegetables. Keep the dog on this diet (with no additives or treats) for a month. If the symptoms of food allergy or intolerance disappear, it is quite likely that your dog has a food allergy.

Don't think that the single ingredient cured the problem. You still must find a suitable diet and ascertain which ingredient in the old diet was objectionable. This is most easily done by adding ingredients to the new diet one at a time. Let the dog stay on the modified diet for a month before you add another ingredient. Eventually, you will determine the ingredient that caused the adverse reaction.

An alternative method is to carefully study the ingredients in the diet to which your dog is allergic or intolerant. Identify the main ingredient in this diet

CARETAKER OF TEETH
You are your dog's caretaker and his dentist. Vets warn that plaque and tartar buildup on the teeth will damage the gums and allow bacteria to enter the dog's bloodstream, causing serious damage to the animal's vital organs. Studies show that over 50 percent of dogs have some form of gum disease before age three. Daily or weekly tooth cleaning (with a brush or soft gauze pad wipes) can add to your dog's life.

and eliminate the main ingredient by buying a different food that does not have that ingredient. Keep experimenting until the symptoms disappear after one month on the new diet.

EXTERNAL PARASITES

FLEAS

Of all the problems to which
dogs are prone, none is more
well known and frustrating than
fleas. Flea infestation is relatively
simple to cure but difficult to
prevent. Parasites that are
harboured inside the body are a
bit more difficult to eradicate but
they are easier to control.

   To control flea infestation,
you have to understand the flea's
life cycle. Fleas are often thought
of as a summertime problem, but
centrally heated homes have
changed the patterns and fleas
can be found at any time of the
year. The most effective method
of flea control is a two-stage
approach: one stage to kill the

adult fleas, and the other to
control the development of pre-
adult fleas. Unfortunately, no
single active ingredient is
effective against all stages of the
life cycle.

LIFE CYCLE STAGES

During its life, a flea will pass
through four life stages: egg, larva,
pupa and adult. The adult stage is

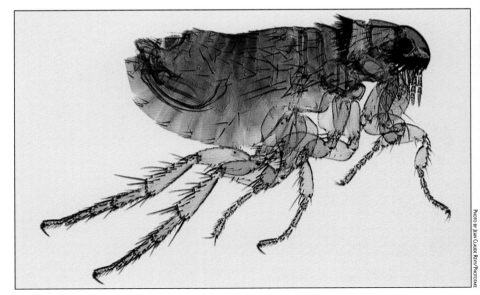

INSECT GROWTH REGULATOR (IGR)

Two types of products should be used when treating fleas—a product to treat the pet and a product to treat the home. Adult fleas represent less than 1% of the flea population. The pre-adult fleas (eggs, larvae and pupae) represent more than 99% of the flea population and are found in the environment; it is in the case of pre-adult fleas that products containing an Insect Growth Regulator (IGR) should be used in the home.

IGRs are a new class of compounds used to prevent the development of insects. They do not kill the insect outright, but instead use the insect's biology against it to stop it from completing its growth. Products that contain methoprene are the world's first and leading IGRs. Used to control fleas and other insects, this type of IGR will stop flea larvae from developing and protect the house for up to seven months.

THE LIFE CYCLE OF THE FLEA

Eggs are laid on the dog, usually in quantities of about 20 or 30, several times a day. The female adult flea must have a blood meal before each egg-laying session. When first laid, the eggs will cling to the dog's hair, as the eggs are still moist. However, they will quickly dry out and fall from the dog, especially if the dog moves around or scratches. Many eggs will fall off in the dog's favourite area or an area in which he spends a lot of time, such as his bed.

Once the eggs fall from the dog onto the carpet or furniture, they will hatch into larvae. This takes from one to ten days. Larvae are not particularly mobile and will usually travel only a few inches from where they hatch. However, they do have a tendency to move away from light and heavy traffic— under furniture and behind doors are common places to find high quantities of flea larvae.

The flea larvae feed on dead the most visible and irritating stage of the flea life cycle, and this is why the majority of flea-control products concentrate on this stage. The fact is that adult fleas account for only 1% of the total flea population, and the other 99% exist in pre-adult stages, i.e. eggs, larvae and pupae. The pre-adult stages are barely visible to the naked eye.

FLEA KILLERS

Flea-killers are poisonous. You should not spray these toxic chemicals on areas of a dog's body that he licks, on his genitals or on his face. Flea killers taken internally are a better answer, but check with your vet in case internal therapy is not advised for your dog.

The Life Cycle of the Flea

Eggs

Larvae

Pupa

Adult

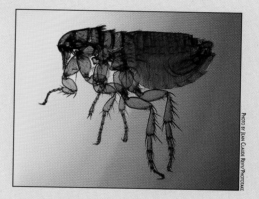

Photo by Jean Claude Revy/Phototake

organic matter, including adult flea faeces, until they are ready to change into adult fleas. Fleas will usually remain as larvae for around seven days. After this period, the larvae will pupate into protective pupae. While inside the pupae, the larvae will undergo metamorphosis and change into adult fleas. This can take as little time as a few days, but the adult fleas can remain inside the pupae waiting to hatch for up to two years. The pupae are signalled to hatch by certain stimuli, such as physical pressure—the pupae's being stepped on, heat from an animal lying on the pupae or increased carbon dioxide levels and vibrations—indicating that a suitable host is available.

Once hatched, the adult flea must feed within a few days. Once the adult flea finds a host, it will not leave voluntarily. It only becomes dislodged by grooming or the host animal's scratching. The adult flea will remain on the host for the duration of its life unless forcibly removed.

A LOOK AT FLEAS

Fleas have been around for millions of years and have adapted to changing host animals. They are able to go through a complete life cycle in less than one month or they can extend their lives to almost two years by remaining as pupae or cocoons. They do not need blood or any other food for up to 20 months.

They have been measured as being able to jump 300,000 times and can jump 150 times their length in any direction, including straight up. Those are just a few of the reasons why they are so successful in infesting a dog!

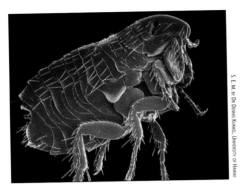

A scanning electron micrograph (S. E. M.) of a dog flea, *Ctenocephalides canis.*

S. E. M. BY DR DENNIS KUNKEL, UNIVERSITY OF HAWAII

actually mimic the fleas' own hormones and stop the eggs and larvae from developing into adult fleas. There are currently no treatments available to attack the pupa stage of the life cycle, so the adult insecticide is used to kill the newly hatched adult fleas before they find a host. Most IGRs are active for many months, while adult insecticides are only active for a few days.

TREATING THE ENVIRONMENT AND THE DOG

Treating fleas should be a two-pronged attack. First, the environment needs to be treated; this includes carpets and furniture, especially the dog's bedding and areas underneath furniture. The environment should be treated with a household spray containing an Insect Growth Regulator (IGR) and an insecticide to kill the adult fleas. Most IGRs are effective against eggs and larvae; they

Dwight R Kuhn's magnificent action photo, showing a flea jumping from a dog's back.

EN GARDE: CATCHING FLEAS OFF GUARD!

Consider the following ways to arm yourself against fleas:

- Add a small amount of pennyroyal or eucalyptus oil to your dog's bath. These natural remedies repel fleas.
- Supplement your dog's food with fresh garlic (minced or grated) and a hearty amount of brewer's yeast, both of which ward off fleas.
- Use a flea comb on your dog daily. Submerge fleas in a cup of bleach to kill them quickly.
- Confine the dog to only a few rooms to limit the spread of fleas in the home.
- Vacuum daily...and get all of the crevices! Dispose of the bag every few days until the problem is under control.
- Wash your dog's bedding daily. Cover cushions where your dog sleeps with towels, and wash the towels often.

PHOTO BY DWIGHT R KUHN

When treating with a household spray, it is a good idea to vacuum before applying the product. This stimulates as many pupae as possible to hatch into adult fleas. The vacuum cleaner should also be treated with an

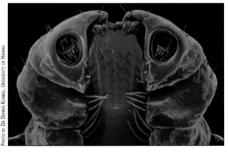

insecticide to prevent the eggs and larvae that have been hoovered into the vacuum bag from hatching.

The second stage of treatment is to apply an adult insecticide to the dog. Traditionally, this would be in the form of a collar or a spray, but more recent innovations include digestible insecticides that poison the fleas when they ingest the dog's blood. Alternatively, there are drops that, when placed on the back of the animal's neck, spread throughout the fur and skin to kill adult fleas.

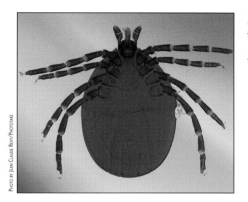

An uncommon dog tick of the genus *Ixode*. Magnified 10x.

TICKS AND MITES

Though not as common as fleas, ticks and mites are found all over the tropical and temperate world. They don't bite, like fleas; they harpoon. They dig their sharp proboscis (nose) into the dog's skin and drink the blood. Their only food and drink is dog's blood. Dogs can get Lyme disease, Rocky Mountain spotted fever (normally found in the US only), paralysis and many other diseases from ticks and mites. They may live where fleas are

The head of a dog tick, *Dermacentor variabilis*, enlarged and coloured for effect.

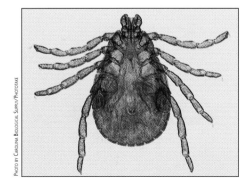

A brown dog tick, *Rhipicephalus sanguineus*, is an uncommon but annoying tick found on dogs.

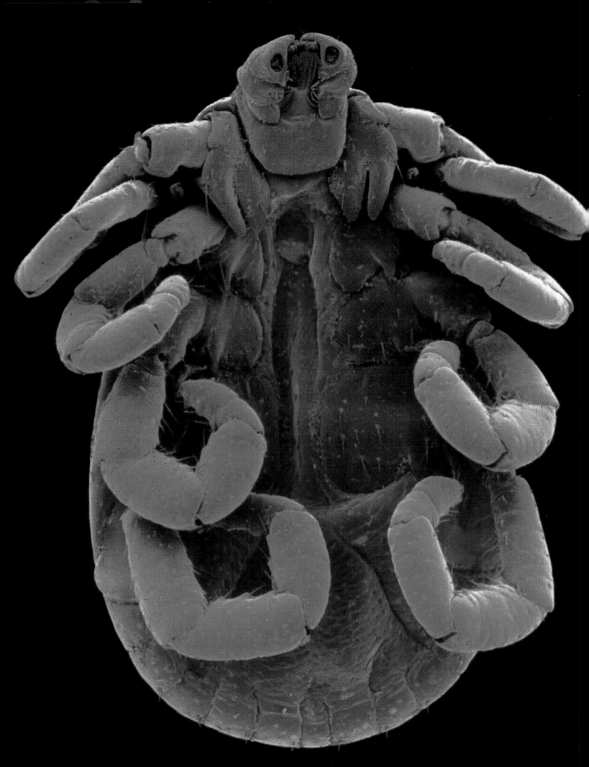

found and they like to hide in cracks or seams in walls wherever dogs live. They are controlled the same way fleas are controlled.

The dog tick, *Dermacentor variabilis*, may well be the most common dog tick in many geographical areas, especially

Human lice look like dog lice; the two are closely related.

PHOTO BY DWIGHT R. KUHN

those areas where the climate is hot and humid.

Most dog ticks have life expectancies of a week to six months, depending upon climatic conditions. They can neither jump nor fly, but they can crawl slowly and can range up to 5 metres (16 feet) to reach a sleeping or unsuspecting dog.

DEER TICK CROSSING

The great outdoors may be fun for your dog, but it also is a home to dangerous ticks. Deer ticks carry a bacterium known as *Borrelia burgdorferi* and are most active in the autumn and spring. When infections are caught early, penicillin and tetracycline are effective antibiotics, but if left untreated the bacteria may cause neurological, kidney and cardiac problems as well as long-term trouble with walking and painful joints.

MANGE

Mites cause a skin irritation called mange. Some are contagious, like *Cheyletiella*, ear mites, scabies and chiggers. Mites that cause ear-mite infestations are usually controlled with Lindane, which can only be administered by a vet, followed by Tresaderm at home.

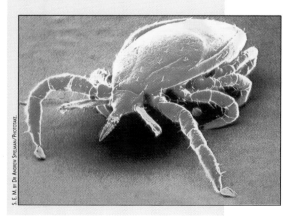

S.E.M. BY DR ANDREW SPIELMAN/PHOTOTAKE.

Opposite page: The dog tick, *Dermacentor variabilis*, is probably the most common tick found on dogs. Look at the strength in its eight legs! No wonder it's hard to detach them.

The roundworm, *Rhabditis*. The roundworm can infect both dogs and humans.

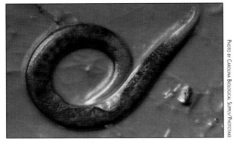

The common roundworm, *Ascaris lumbricoides*.

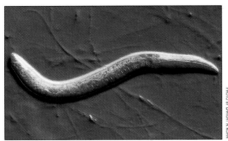

ROUNDWORMS

Average-size dogs can pass 1,360,000 roundworm eggs every day. For example, if there were only 1 million dogs in the world, the world would be saturated with 1,300 metric tonnes of dog faeces. These faeces would contain 15,000,000,000 roundworm eggs.

Up to 31% of home gardens and children's play boxes in the US contain roundworm eggs.

Flushing dog's faeces down the toilet is not a safe practice because the usual sewage treatments do not destroy roundworm eggs.

Infected puppies start shedding roundworm eggs at 3 weeks of age. They can be infected by their mother's milk.

DEWORMING

Ridding your puppy of worms is *very important* because certain worms that puppies carry, such as tapeworms and roundworms, can infect humans.

Breeders initiate deworming programmes at or about four weeks of age. The routine is repeated every two or three weeks until the puppy is three months old. The breeder from whom you obtained your puppy should provide you with the complete details of the deworming programme.

Your veterinary surgeon can prescribe and monitor the programme of deworming for you. The usual programme is treating the puppy every 15–20 days until the puppy is positively worm-free. It is advised that you only treat your puppy with drugs that are recommended professionally.

It is essential that your dog be treated for mange as quickly as possible because some forms of mange are transmissible to people.

INTERNAL PARASITES

Most animals—fishes, birds and mammals, including dogs and humans—have worms and other parasites that live inside their bodies. According to Dr Herbert R Axelrod, the fish pathologist, there are two kinds of parasites:

dumb and smart. The smart parasites live in peaceful cooperation with their hosts (symbiosis), while the dumb parasites kill their hosts. Most of the worm infections are relatively easy to control. If they are not controlled, they weaken the host dog to the point that other medical problems occur, but they are not dumb parasites.

ROUNDWORMS

The roundworms that infect dogs are scientifically known as *Toxocara canis*. They live in the dog's intestines. The worms shed eggs continually. It has been estimated that a dog produces about 150 grammes of faeces every day. Each gramme of faeces averages 10,000–12,000 eggs of roundworms. There are no known areas in which dogs roam that do not contain roundworm eggs. The greatest danger of roundworms is that they infect people too! It is wise to have your dog tested regularly for roundworms.

Pigs also have roundworm infections that can be passed to humans and dogs. The typical roundworm parasite is called *Ascaris lumbricoides.*

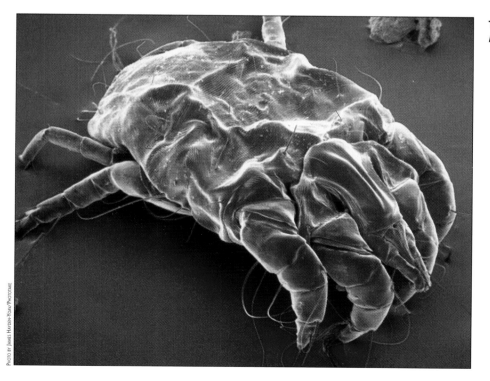

The mange mite, *Psoroptes bovis.*

PHOTO BY JAMES HAYDEN-YOAV/PHOTOTAKE

The roundworm *Rhabditis.*

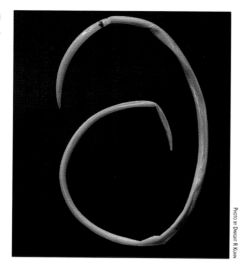

PHOTO BY DWIGHT R KUHN

HOOKWORMS

Right: Male and female hookworms. *Ancylostoma caninum* are uncommonly found in pet or show dogs in Britain.

Below: The infective stage of the hookworm larva.

The worm *Ancylostoma caninum* is commonly called the dog hookworm. It is also dangerous to humans and cats. It has teeth by which it attaches itself to the intestines of the dog. It changes the site of its attachment about six times a day and the dog loses blood from each detachment, possibly causing iron-deficiency anaemia. Hookworms are easily purged from the dog with many medications. Milbemycin oxime, which also serves as a heartworm preventative in Collies, can be used for this purpose.

In Britain the 'temperate climate' hookworm (*Uncinaria stenocephala*) is rarely found in pet or show dogs, but can occur in hunting packs, racing Greyhounds and sheepdogs because the worms can be prevalent wherever dogs are exercised regularly on grassland.

TAPEWORMS

There are many species of tapeworm. They are carried by fleas! The dog eats the flea and starts the tapeworm cycle. Humans can also be infected with tapeworms, so don't eat fleas! Fleas are so small that your dog could pass them onto your hands, your plate or your food and thus make it possible for you to ingest a flea that is carrying tapeworm eggs.

While tapeworm infection is

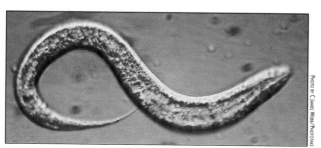

PHOTO BY C JAMES WEBB/PHOTOTAKE

PHOTO BY DWIGHT R KUHN

TAPEWORMS

Humans, rats, squirrels, foxes, coyotes, wolves, and domestic dogs are all susceptible to tapeworm infection. Except in humans, tapeworms are usually not a fatal infection. Infected individuals can harbour a thousand parasitic worms.

Tapeworms have two sexes—male and female (many other worms have only one sex—male and female in the same worm).

If dogs eat infected rats or mice, they get the tapeworm disease. One month after attaching to a dog's intestine, the worm starts shedding eggs. These eggs are infective immediately. Infective eggs can live for a few months without a host animal.

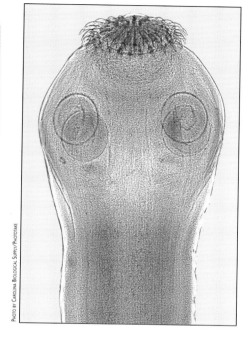

PHOTO BY CAROLINA BIOLOGICAL SUPPLY/PHOTOTAKE

The head and rostellum (the round prominence on the scolex) of a tapeworm, which infects dogs and humans.

not life-threatening in dogs (smart parasite!), it can be the cause of a very serious liver disease for humans. About 50 percent of the humans infected with *Echinococcus multilocularis*, a type of tapeworm that causes alveolar hydatis, perish.

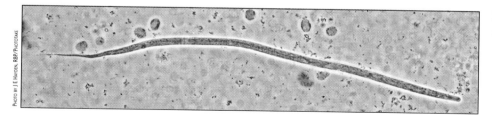

PHOTO BY J E HAYDEN, RBP/PHOTOTAKE

Heartworm, *Dirofilaria immitis*.

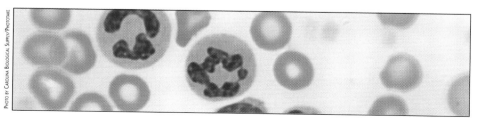

PHOTO BY CAROLINA BIOLOGICAL SUPPLY/PHOTOTAKE

Magnified heartworm larvae, *Dirofilaria immitis*.

First Aid at a Glance

Burns
Place the affected area under cool water; use ice if only a small area is burnt.

Bee/Insect bites
Apply ice to relieve swelling; antihistamine dosed properly.

Animal bites
Clean any bleeding area; apply pressure until bleeding subsides; go to the vet.

Spider bites
Use cold compress and a pressurised pack to inhibit venom's spreading.

Antifreeze poisoning
Induce vomiting with hydrogen peroxide. Seek *immediate* veterinary help!

Fish hooks
Removal best handled by vet; hook must be cut in order to remove.

Snake bites
Pack ice around bite; contact vet quickly; identify snake for proper antivenin.

Car accident
Move dog from roadway with blanket; seek veterinary aid.

Shock
Calm the dog, keep him warm; seek immediate veterinary help.

Nosebleed
Apply cold compress to the nose; apply pressure to any visible abrasion.

Bleeding
Apply pressure above the area; treat wound by applying a cotton pack.

Heat stroke
Submerge dog in cold bath; cool down with fresh air and water; go to the vet.

Frostbite/Hypothermia
Warm the dog with a warm bath, electric blankets or hot water bottles.

Abrasions
Clean the wound and wash out thoroughly with fresh water; apply antiseptic.

 Remember: an injured dog may attempt to bite a helping hand from fear and confusion. Always muzzle the dog before trying to offer assistance.

HEARTWORMS

Heartworms are thin, extended worms up to 30 cms (12 ins) long, which live in a dog's heart and the major blood vessels surrounding it. Dogs may have up to 200 worms. Symptoms may be loss of energy, loss of appetite, coughing, the development of a pot belly and anaemia.

Heartworms are transmitted by mosquitoes. The mosquito drinks the blood of an infected dog and takes in larvae with the blood. The larvae, called microfilaria, develop within the body of the mosquito and are passed on to the next dog bitten after the larvae mature. It takes two to three weeks for the larvae to develop to the infective stage within the body of the mosquito. Dogs should be treated at about six weeks of age, and maintained on a prophylactic dose given monthly.

Blood testing for heartworms is not necessarily indicative of how seriously your dog is infected. This is a dangerous disease. Although heartworm is a problem for dogs in America, Australia, Asia and Central Europe, dogs in the United Kingdom are not currently affected by heartworm.

The heart of a dog infected with canine heartworm, *Dirofilaria immitis.*

HOMEOPATHY:
an alternative
to conventional
medicine

'Less is Most'

Using this principle, the strength
of a homeopathic remedy is
measured by the number of
serial dilutions that were
undertaken to create it. The
greater the number of serial
dilutions, the greater the
strength of the homeopathic
remedy. The potency of a
remedy that has been made by
making a dilution of 1 part in
100 parts (or 1/100) is 1c or 1cH.
If this remedy is subjected to a
series of further dilutions, each
one being 1/100, a more dilute
and stronger remedy is
produced. If the remedy is
diluted in this way six times, it is
called 6c or 6cH. A dilution of 6c
is 1 part in 1,000,000,000,000. In
general, higher potencies in
more frequent doses are better
for acute symptoms and lower
potencies in more infrequent
doses are more useful for
chronic, long-standing problems.

CURING OUR DOGS NATURALLY

Holistic medicine means treating the whole animal as a unique, perfect living being. Generally, holistic treatments do not suppress the symptoms that the body naturally produces, as do most medications prescribed by conventional doctors and vets. Holistic methods seek to cure disease by regaining balance and harmony in the patient's environment. Some of these methods include use of nutritional therapy, herbs, flower essences, aromatherapy, acupuncture, massage, chiropractic and, of course, the most popular holistic approach, homeopathy.

Homeopathy is a theory or system of treating illness with small doses of substances which, if administered in larger quantities, would produce the symptoms that the patient already has. This approach is often described as 'like cures like.' Although modern veterinary medicine is geared toward the 'quick fix,' homeopathy relies on the belief that, given the time, the body is able to heal itself and return to its natural, healthy state.

Choosing a remedy to cure a problem in our dogs is the difficult part of homeopathy. Consult with your veterinary surgeon for a professional diagnosis of your dog's symptoms. Often these symptoms

Using 'Like to Treat Like'

Unlike conventional medicines that suppress symptoms, homeopathic remedies treat illnesses with small doses of substances that, if administered in larger quantities, would produce the symptoms that the patient already has. While the same homeopathic remedy can be used to treat different symptoms in different dogs, here are some interesting remedies and their uses.

Apis Mellifica
(made from honey bee venom) can be used for allergies or to reduce swelling that occurs in acutely infected kidneys.

Diesel Smoke
can be used to help control travel sickness.

Calcarea Fluorica
(made from calcium fluoride, which helps harden bone structure) can be useful in treating hard lumps in tissues.

Natrum Muriaticum
(made from common salt, sodium chloride) is useful in treating thin, thirsty dogs.

Nitricum Acidum
(made from nitric acid) is used for symptoms you would expect to see from contact with acids, such as lesions, especially where the skin joins the linings of body orifices or openings such as the lips and nostrils.

Symphytum
(made from the herb Knitbone, *Symphytum officinale*) is used to encourage bones to heal.

Urtica Urens
(made from the common stinging nettle) is used in treating painful, irritating rashes.

require immediate conventional care. If your vet is willing, and knowledgeable, you may attempt a homeopathic remedy. Be aware that cortisone prevents homeopathic remedies from working. There are hundreds of possibilities and combinations to cure many problems in dogs, from basic physical problems such as excessive moulting, fleas or other parasites, unattractive doggy odour, bad breath, upset tummy, obesity, dry, oily or dull coat, diarrhoea, ear problems or eye discharge (including tears and dry or mucousy matter), to behavioural abnormalities, such as fear of loud noises, habitual licking, poor appetite, excessive barking and various phobias. From alumina to zincum metallicum, the remedies span the planet and the imagination...from flowers and weeds to chemicals, insect droppings, diesel smoke and volcanic ash.

HOMEOPATHIC REMEDIES FOR YOUR DOG

Symptom/Ailment	Possible Remedy
ALLERGIES	Apis Mellifica 30c, Astacus Fluviatilis 6c, Pulsatilla 30c, Urtica Urens 6c
ALOPAECIA	Alumina 30c, Lycopodium 30c, Sepia 30c, Thallium 6c
ANAL GLANDS (BLOCKED)	Hepar Sulphuris Calcareum 30c, Sanicula 6c, Silicea 6c
ARTHRITIS	Rhus Toxicodendron 6c, Bryonia Alba 6c
CATARACT	Calcarea Carbonica 6c, Conium Maculatum 6c, Phosphorus 30c, Silicea 30c
CONSTIPATION	Alumina 6c, Carbo Vegetabilis 30c, Graphites 6c, Nitricum Acidum 30c, Silicea 6c
COUGHING	Aconitum Napellus 6c, Belladonna 30c, Hyoscyamus Niger 30c, Phosphorus 30c
DIARRHOEA	Arsenicum Album 30c, Aconitum Napellus 6c, Chamomilla 30c, Mercurius Corrosivus 30c
DRY EYE	Zincum Metallicum 30c
EAR PROBLEMS	Aconitum Napellus 30c, Belladonna 30c, Hepar Sulphuris 30c, Tellurium 30c, Psorinum 200c
EYE PROBLEMS	Borax 6c, Aconitum Napellus 30c, Graphites 6c, Staphysagria 6c, Thuja Occidentalis 30c
GLAUCOMA	Aconitum Napellus 30c, Apis Mellifica 6c, Phosphorus 30c
HEAT STROKE	Belladonna 30c, Gelsemium Sempervirens 30c, Sulphur 30c
HICCOUGHS	Cinchona Deficinalis 6c
HIP DYSPLASIA	Colocynthis 6c, Rhus Toxicodendron 6c, Bryonia Alba 6c
INCONTINENCE	Argentum Nitricum 6c, Causticum 30c, Conium Maculatum 30c, Pulsatilla 30c, Sepia 30c
INSECT BITES	Apis Mellifica 30c, Cantharis 30c, Hypericum Perforatum 6c, Urtica Urens 30c
ITCHING	Alumina 30c, Arsenicum Album 30c, Carbo Vegetabilis 30c, Hypericum Perforatum 6c, Mezerium 6c, Sulphur 30c
KENNEL COUGH	Drosera 6c, Ipecacuanha 30c
MASTITIS	Apis Mellifica 30c, Belladonna 30c, Urtica Urens 1m
PATELLAR LUXATION	Gelsemium Sempervirens 6c, Rhus Toxicodendron 6c
PENIS PROBLEMS	Aconitum Napellus 30c, Hepar Sulphuris Calcareum 30c, Pulsatilla 30c, Thuja Occidentalis 6c
PUPPY TEETHING	Calcarea Carbonica 6c, Chamomilla 6c, Phytolacca 6c
TRAVEL SICKNESS	Cocculus 6c, Petroleum 6c

Get Well Soon

You don't need a DVR or a BVMA to provide good TLC to your sick or recovering dog, but you do need to pay attention to some details that normally wouldn't bother him. The following tips will aid Fido's recovery and get him back on his paws again:

- Keep his space free of irritating smells, like heavy perfumes and air fresheners.
- Rest is the best medicine! Avoid harsh lighting that will prevent your dog from sleeping. Shade him from bright sunlight during the day and dim the lights in the evening.
- Keep the noise level down. Animals are more sensitive to sound when they are sick.

- Be attentive to any necessary temperature adjustments. A dog with a fever needs a cool room and cold liquids. A bitch that is whelping or recovering from surgery will be more comfortable in a warm room, consuming warm liquids and food.
- You wouldn't send a sick child back to school early, so don't rush your dog back into a full routine until he seems absolutely ready.

Recognising a Sick Dog

Unlike colicky babies and cranky children, our canine charges cannot tell us when they are feeling ill. Therefore, there are a number of signs that owners can identify to know that their dogs are not feeling well.

Take note for physical manifestations such as:

- unusual, bad odour, including bad breath
- excessive moulting
- wax in the ears, chronic ear irritation
- oily, flaky, dull haircoat
- mucous, tearing or similar discharge in the eyes
- fleas or mites
- mucous in stool, diarrhoea
- sensitivity to petting or handling
- licking at paws, scratching face, etc.

Keep an eye out for behavioural changes as well including:

- lethargy, idleness
- lack of patience or general irritability
- lack of appetite, digestive problems
- phobias (fear of people, loud noises, etc.)
- strange behaviour, suspicion, fear
- coprophagia
- more frequent barking
- whimpering, crying

Number-One Killer Disease in Dogs: CANCER

In every age there is a word associated with a disease or plague that causes humans to shudder. In the 21st century, that word is 'cancer.' Just as cancer is the leading cause of death in humans, it claims nearly half the lives of dogs that die from a natural disease as well as half the dogs that die over the age of ten years.

Described as a genetic disease, cancer becomes a greater risk as the dog ages. Veterinary surgeons and dog owners have become increasingly aware of the threat of cancer to dogs. Statistics reveal that one dog in every five will develop cancer, the most common of which is skin cancer. Many cancers, including prostate, ovarian and breast cancer, can be avoided by spaying and neutering our dogs by the age of six months.

Early detection of cancer can save or extend your dog's life, so it is absolutely vital for owners to have their dogs examined by a qualified veterinary surgeon or oncologist immediately upon detection of any abnormality. Certain dietary guidelines have also proven to reduce the onset and spread of cancer. Foods based on fish rather than beef, due to the presence of Omega-3 fatty acids, are recommended. Other amino acids such as glutamine have significant benefits for canines,

RECOGNISE CANCER WARNING SIGNS

Since early detection can possibly rescue your dog from becoming a cancer statistic, it is essential for owners to recognise the possible signs and seek the assistance of a qualified professional.

- Abnormal bumps or lumps that continue to grow
- Bleeding or discharge from any body cavity
- Persistent stiffness or lameness
- Recurrent sores or sores that do not heal
- Inappetence
- Breathing difficulties
- Weight loss
- Bad breath or odours
- General malaise and fatigue
- Eating and swallowing problems
- Difficulty urinating and defecating

particularly those breeds that show a greater susceptibility to cancer.

Cancer management and treatments promise hope for future generations of canines. Since the disease is genetic, breeders should never breed a dog whose parents, grandparents and any related siblings have developed cancer. It is difficult to know whether to exclude an otherwise healthy dog from a breeding programme as the disease does not manifest itself until the dog's senior years.

Disease	Percentage
Cancer	47%
Heart disease	12%
Kidney disease	7%
Epilepsy	4%
Liver disease	4%
Bloat	3%
Diabetes	3%
Stroke	2%
Cushing's disease	2%
Immune diseases	2%
Other causes	14%

The Ten Most Common Fatal Diseases in Pure-bred Dogs

CDS: COGNITIVE DYSFUNCTION SYNDROME
'OLD-DOG SYNDROME'

SYMPTOMS OF CDS

FREQUENT TOILET ACCIDENTS
- Urinates in the house.
- Defecates in the house.
- Doesn't signal that he wants to go out.

SLEEP PATTERNS
- Moves much more slowly.
- Sleeps more than normal during the day.
- Sleeps less during the night.

CONFUSION
- Goes outside and just stands there.
- Appears confused with a faraway look in his eyes.
- Hides more often.
- Doesn't recognise friends.
- Doesn't come when called.
- Walks around listlessly and without a destination.

FAILS TO RESPOND TO SOCIAL STIMULI
- Comes to people less frequently, whether called or not.
- Doesn't tolerate petting for more than a short time.
- Doesn't come to the door when you return home.

There are many ways to evaluate old-dog syndrome. Veterinary surgeons have defined CDS (cognitive dysfunction syndrome) as the gradual deterioration of cognitive abilities. These are indicated by changes in the dog's behaviour. When a dog changes its routine response, and maladies have been eliminated as the cause of these behavioural changes, then CDS is the usual diagnosis.

More than half the dogs over eight years old suffer from some form of CDS. The older the dog, the more chance it has of suffering from CDS. In humans, doctors often dismiss the CDS behavioural changes as part of 'winding down.'

There are four major signs of CDS: the dog has frequent toilet accidents inside the home, sleeps much more or much less than normal, acts confused and fails to respond to social stimuli.

Showing Your
ITALIAN SPINONE

When you buy your Spinone, you will make it clear to the breeder whether you want one just as a loveable companion and pet, or if you hope to be buying an Italian Spinone with show prospects. No reputable breeder will sell you a young puppy and tell you that it is *definitely* of show quality, for so much can go wrong during the early months of a puppy's development. If you plan to show, what you will hopefully have acquired is a puppy with 'show potential.'

To the novice, exhibiting a Spinone in the show ring may look easy, but it takes a lot of hard work and devotion to do top winning at a show such as the prestigious Crufts Dog Show, not to mention a little luck too!

The first concept that the canine novice learns when watching a dog show is that each dog first competes against members of its own breed. Once the judge has selected the best member of each breed (Best of Breed), provided that the show is judged on a Group system, that chosen dog will compete with other dogs in its group. Finally, the best of each group will compete for Best in Show and Reserve Best in Show.

The second concept that you must understand is that the dogs are not actually compared against one another. The judge compares each dog against its breed standard, which is a written description of the ideal specimen of the breed. While some early breed standards were indeed based on specific dogs that were famous or popular, many

INFORMATION ON CLUBS

You can get information about dog shows from kennel clubs and breed clubs:

Fédération Cynologique Internationale
14, rue Leopold II, B-6530 Thuin, Belgium
www.fci.be

The Kennel Club
1-5 Clarges St., Piccadilly, London W1Y 8AB, UK
www.the-kennel-club.org.uk

American Kennel Club
5580 Centerview Dr., Raleigh, NC 27606-3390
USA
www.akc.org

Canadian Kennel Club
89 Skyway Ave., Suite 100, Etobicoke, Ontario
M9W 6R4 Canada
www.ckc.ca

dedicated enthusiasts say that a perfect specimen, as described in the standard, has never walked into a show ring, has never been bred and, to the woe of dog breeders around the globe, does not exist. Breeders attempt to get as close to this ideal as possible with every litter, but theoretically the 'perfect' dog is so elusive that it is impossible. (And if the 'perfect' dog were born, breeders and judges would never agree that it was indeed 'perfect.')

If you are interested in exploring the world of dog showing, your best bet is to join your local breed club. These clubs often host both Championship and Open Shows, and sometimes Match meetings and special events, all of which could be of interest, even if you are only an onlooker. Clubs also send out newsletters, and some organise training days and seminars in order that people may learn more about their chosen breed. To locate the breed club closest to you, contact The Kennel Club, the ruling body for the British dog world. The Kennel Club governs not only conformation shows but also working trials, obedience shows, agility trials and field trials. The Kennel Club furnishes the rules and regulations for all of these events plus general dog registration and other basic requirements of dog ownership. Its annual show, called the Crufts Dog Show, held in Birmingham, is the largest benched show in England. Every year over 20,000 of the UK's

SHOW QUALITY SHOWS

While you may purchase a puppy in the hope of having a successful career in the show ring, it is impossible to tell, at eight to ten weeks of age, whether your dog will be a contender. Some promising pups end up with minor to serious faults that prevent them from taking home a Best of Breed award, but this certainly does not mean they can't be the best of companions for you and your family. To find out if your potential show dog is show quality, enter him in a match to see how a judge evaluates him. You may also take him back to your breeder as he matures to see what he might advise.

The handler 'stacks' or 'stands' the dog in the show ring...and a sure way to keep him in position is to focus his attention on a tasty titbit.

best dogs qualify to participate in this marvellous show, which lasts four days.

The Kennel Club governs many different kinds of shows in Great Britain, Australia, South Africa and beyond. At the most competitive and prestigious of these shows, the Championship Shows, a dog can earn Challenge Certificates (CCs), and thereby become a Show Champion or a Champion. A dog must earn three Challenge Certificates under three different judges to earn the prefix of 'Sh Ch' or 'Ch.' Some breeds must also qualify in a field trial in order to gain the title of full Champion, and the Italian Spinone is one such breed. Challenge Certificates are awarded

to a very small percentage of the dogs competing, and dogs that are already Champions compete with others for these coveted CCs. The number of Challenge Certificates awarded in any one year is based upon the total number of dogs in each breed entered for competition.

There are three types of Championship Shows: an all-breed General Championship Show for all Kennel-Club-recognised breeds; a Group Championship Show, which is limited to breeds within one of the groups; and a Breed Show, which is usually confined to a single breed. The Kennel Club determines which breeds at which Championship Shows will have the opportunity to earn Challenge Certificates (or tickets). Serious exhibitors often will opt not to participate if the tickets are withheld at a particular show. This policy makes earning championships even more difficult to accomplish.

Open Shows are generally less competitive and are frequently used as 'practice shows' for young dogs. There are hundreds of Open Shows each year that can be delightful social events and are great first show experiences for the novice. Even if you're considering just watching a show to wet your paws, an Open Show is a great choice.

While Championship and

Open Shows are most important for the beginner to understand, there are other types of shows in which the interested dog owner can participate. Training clubs sponsor Matches that can be entered on the day of the show for a nominal fee. In these introductory-level exhibitions, two dogs' names are pulled out of a hat and 'matched,' the winner of that match goes on to the next round and eventually only one dog is left undefeated.

Exemption Shows are much more light-hearted affairs with usually only four pedigree classes and several 'fun' classes, all of which can be entered on the day of the show. Exemption Shows are sometimes held in conjunction with small agricultural shows and the proceeds must be given to a charity. Limited Shows are also available in small number. Entry is restricted to members of the club that hosts the show, although one can usually join the club when making an entry.

Before you actually step into the ring, you would be well advised to sit back and observe the judge's ring procedure. If it is your first time in the ring, do not be over-anxious and run to the front of the line. It is much better to stand back and study how the exhibitor in front of you is performing. The judge asks each handler to 'stand' the dog, hopefully showing the dog off to his best advantage. The judge will observe the dog from a distance and from different angles, and approach the dog to check his teeth, overall structure, alertness and muscle tone, as well as consider how well the dog 'conforms' to the standard. Most importantly, the judge will have

TIDINESS COUNTS

Surely you've spent hours grooming your dog to perfection for the show ring, but don't forget about yourself! While the dog should be the centre of attention, it is important that you also appear clean and tidy. Wear smart, appropriate clothes and comfortable shoes in a colour that contrasts with your dog's coat. Look and act like a professional.

Spinone and handler participating in a hunting trial. This is perhaps the most enjoyable type of competition for this talented field dog.

the exhibitor move the dog around the ring in some pattern that he or she should specify (another advantage to not going first, but always listen since some judges change their directions—and the judge is always right!). Finally, the judge will give the dog one last look before moving on to the next exhibitor.

If you are not in the top three at your first show, do not be discouraged. Be patient and consistent, and you may eventually find yourself in the winning line-up. Remember that the winners were once in your shoes and have devoted many hours and much money to earn the placement. If you find that your dog is losing every time and never getting a nod, it may be time to consider a different dog sport or to

just enjoy your Spinone as a pet.

Virtually all countries with a recognised speciality breed club (sometimes called a 'parent' club) offer show conformation competition specifically for and among Spinoni. Under direction of the club, other special events for hunting, tracking, obedience and agility may be offered as well, whether for titling or just for fun.

FIELD AND GUNDOG WORK

Most Spinoni excel at the business of finding and retrieving game—hunting! A well-trained Spinone, a pointer by trade, is a joy on rough shoots and an asset when picking up behind the guns.

NO SHOW

Never show a dog that is sick, lame or recovering from surgery or infection. Not only will this put your own dog under a tremendous amount of stress, but you will also put other dogs at risk of contracting any illness your dog has. Likewise, bitches who are in heat will distract and disrupt the performances of males who are competing, and bitches that are pregnant will likely be stressed and exhausted by a long day of showing.

A GENTLEMAN'S SPORT
Whether or not your dog wins top honours, showing is a pleasant social event. Sometimes, one may meet a troublemaker or nasty exhibitor, but these people should be ignored and forgotten. In the extremely rare case that someone threatens or harasses you or your dog, you can lodge a complaint with The Kennel Club. This should be done with extreme prudence. Complaints are investigated seriously and should never be filed on a whim.

When picking up, the dog and the handler are assigned an area to cover and clear of birds. The dogs push out the game as well as retrieve the fallen birds. Working in a natural environment with his instincts in high gear, the Spinone can revel in his natural heritage and clearly enjoys every working minute.

In rough shooting, the dog and handler work alone as a single team, hunting, shooting and retrieving game. The dogs visibly love their job, and their owners enjoy seeing the dogs work as much as, if not more than, the actual shoot. A Spinone can work in the field until around six years of age, which is an impressive field career for any dog.

FIELD TRIALS AND WORKING TESTS

Working tests are frequently used to prepare dogs for field trials, the purpose of which is to heighten the instincts and natural abilities of Gundogs. Live game is not used in working tests. Unlike field trials, working tests do not count towards a dog's record at The Kennel Club, though the same judges often oversee working tests.

Field trials began in England in 1947 and are only moderately popular among dog folk. While breeders of the Gundog breeds concern themselves with the field abilities of their dogs, there is considerably less interest in field trials than in dog shows. Keep in mind that Italian Spinoni must qualify at a field trial to become a full Champion with The Kennel Club. Dogs that do not can never rise above the title Show Champion. The title Champion requires that the dog gain an award at a field trial, be a 'special qualifier' at a field trial or pass a 'special dog show qualifier' judged by a field trial judge on a shooting day.

The first Italian Spinone to become a full Champion was Sentling Zenzero, who did so in December 1998. Ch Sentling Zenzero became an icon for the breed in England, not only the first Champion of the breed in the UK but also a Best in Show winner.

WORKING TRIALS

Working trials can be entered by any well-trained dog of any breed, but Gundogs or Working dogs make up most of the participants. Many dogs that earn the Kennel Club Good Citizen Dog award choose to participate in a working trial. There are five stakes at both Open and Championship levels: Companion Dog (CD), Utility Dog (UD), Working Dog (WD), Tracking Dog (TD) and Patrol Dog (PD). As in conformation shows, dogs compete against a standard and, if the dog reaches the qualifying mark, it obtains a certificate. The exercises are divided into groups, and the dog must achieve at least 70 percent of the allotted score for each exercise in order to qualify. If the dog achieves 80 percent in the Open level, it receives a Certificate of Merit (COM); in the Championship level, it receives a Qualifying Certificate. At the CD stake, dogs must participate in four groups: Control, Stay, Agility and Search (Retrieve and Nosework). At the next three levels, UD, WD and TD, there are only three groups: Control, Agility and Nosework.

The Agility exercises consist of three jumps: a vertical scale up a six-foot wall of planks; a clear jump over a basic three-foot hurdle with a removable top bar; and a long jump across angled planks stretching nine feet.

To earn the UD, WD and TD, dogs must track approximately one-half mile for articles laid from one-half hour to three hours previously. Tracks consist of turns and legs, and fresh ground is used for each participant. The fifth stake, PD, involves teaching manwork, which is not recommended for every breed.

AGILITY TRIALS

Agility trials began in the United Kingdom in 1977 and have since spread around the world, especially to the United States where they are very popular. The handler directs his dog over an obstacle course that includes jumps (such as those used in the working trials), as well as tyres, the dog walk, weave poles, pipe tunnels, collapsed tunnels, etc. The Kennel Club requires that dogs not be trained for agility until they are 12 months old. This dog sport is great fun for dog and owner, and interested owners should join a training club that has obstacles and experienced agility handlers who can introduce you and your dog to the 'ropes' (and tyres, tunnels, etc.).

FÉDÉRATION CYNOLOGIQUE INTERNATIONALE

Established in 1911, the Fédération Cynologique Internationale (FCI) represents the 'world kennel club.' This international body brings uniformity to the breeding, judging and showing of pure-bred dogs. Although the FCI originally included only five European nations: France, Germany, Austria, the Netherlands and Belgium (which remains its headquarters), the organisation today embraces nations on six continents and recognises well over 300 breeds of pure-bred dog.

FCI sponsors both national and international shows. The hosting country determines the judging system and breed standards are always based on the breed's country of origin. Dogs from every country can participate in the impressive FCI shows, the largest of which is the World Dog Show, hosted in a different country each year.

Titles attainable through the FCI include the International Champion, which is the most prestigious; the International Beauty Champion, which is based on aptitude certificates in different countries; and the International Trial Champion, which is based on achievement in obedience trials in different countries.

To become an FCI Champion, a dog must win three CACs

(*Certificat d'Aptitude au Championnat*) at regional or club shows under three different judges who are breed specialists. The title of International Champion is gained by winning four CACIBs (*Certificat d'Aptitude au Championnat International de Beauté*), which are offered only at international shows, with at least a one-year lapse between the first and fourth award.

Besides the World Dog Show and other all-breed shows, you can exhibit your dog at speciality shows held by different breed clubs. Speciality shows may have their own regulations.

The Spinone's function, the essence of the breed, should never be lost on show dogs. It's a wonderful sight to watch this working dog show his powerful gait in the ring.

INDEX

My Italian Spinone

PUT YOUR PUPPY'S FIRST PICTURE HERE

Dog's Name _____

Date _____ Photographer _____